Hannes Gumtau
Wolfgang Kurschatke

Englisch
1. Lernjahr

Grammatik
Rechtschreibung
Wortschatz
Übungstests

MANZ VERLAG MÜNCHEN

Die deutsche Bibliothek – CIP-Einheitsaufnahme

Gumtau/Kurschatke:
Englisch 1.Lernjahr: Grammatik – Rechtschreibung – Wortschatz –
Übungstests / Hannes Gumtau/Wolfgang Kurschatke. –
München: Manz (1995)
ISBN 3-7863-0582-X

1. Auflage 1995

Umschlaggestaltung: Zembsch' Werkstatt, München
Illustrationen, Satz und Layout: Hans Limo Lechner, Pastetten
Gesamtherstellung: Verlag und Druckerei G. J. Manz AG,
München / Dillingen

ISBN 3-7863-0582-X

Inhalt

Vorwort

Liebe Schülerinnen und Schüler,

Übung macht nicht immer den Meister, hilft aber doch, im Unterricht besser zu werden und viele Fehler zu vermeiden. In diesem Buch sind Übungen und Tips systematisch zusammengestellt. Sie beziehen sich auf den Stoff des ersten Lernjahres und behandeln besonders Fehlerquellen, die eure Note leicht in den Keller ziehen können. **Beispiele** und **Merksätze** werden euch an das erinnern, was ihr im Unterricht schon einmal gehört habt, aber – kann ja vorkommen – wieder vergessen habt. Mögliche Stolpersteine sind durch **Ausrufungszeichen** gekennzeichnet.

Wie könntet ihr vorgehen?

Überlegt zunächst, wo euch der Schuh am meisten drückt und wählt dann einen der vier „Lernbereiche“, z.B.,

wenn	ihr Probleme mit Diktaten habt	**Rechtschreibung**
wenn	die Zeiten nicht ganz klar sind	**Grammatik**
wenn	euch die richtigen Wörter fehlen	**Wortschatz**
wenn	ihr mehr Einser möchtet	**Prüfungstraining**

Dann schaut ihr in euren Heften nach, wo sich die meisten Fehler eingeschlichen haben. Die Übungen dazu macht ihr zuerst. Wenn ihr wissen wollt, wie gut die anderen Sachen sitzen, dann arbeitet ihr auch die übrigen Lernbereiche durch.

Schreibt eure Antworten in die Lücken oder freien Zeilen. Für manche Übungen müßt ihr ein Heft benutzen. Keine Sorge, Hinweise findet ihr an den entsprechenden Stellen.

Bestimmt macht es mehr Spaß, die Übungen mit Freundinnen und Freunden zu machen, aber ihr könnt auch in Ruhe allein üben. Wenn ihr mit einer Aufgabe fertig seid, dann könnt ihr eure Eintragungen mit den Lösungsvorschlägen der Autoren vergleichen. Aber zuerst müßt ihr es selber machen, mogeln gilt nicht!

Ganz gleich, ob ihr auf das Gymnasium, die Realschule oder die Gesamtschule geht, in jedem Fall wird euch dieses Buch weiterhelfen. Sollte irgendeines der Themen bei euch in diesem Schuljahr noch nicht drankommen, dann könnt ihr die Seiten einfach überspringen und auf das nächste Jahr vertagen.

Besonders schwierige Übungen haben wir mit einem  gekennzeichnet

Wenn ihr Lust habt, dann schreibt an den Verlag, wie euch dieses Buch gefallen hat und ob es euch zu einer besseren Note verholfen hat. Wir würden uns freuen.

Manz Verlag
Anzinger Straße 15
81671 München

Viel Spaß und viel Erfolg wünschen euch
die Autoren und der Verlag

★ Tips

Lernkartei mit Hilfen zur Grammatik 6
Fachausdrücke 7

1 Artikel – Substantiv

'a' oder 'an' . . . . . *(a bike, an old bike)* 8
Regelmäßiger Plural . . . . . *(girls, boxes, ladies, potatoes)* 9
Unregelmäßiger Plural . . . . *(men, mice)* 10
This / that – these / those
im Singular und Plural 11
-s Genitiv . . . . . *(Peter's family, the Potters' house)* 12
of-Genitiv . . . . . *(the name of the street)* 13

2 Pronomen – Mengenbezeichnungen

Personalpronomen . . . . . *(I, he; me, him)* 15
Possessivpronomen . . . . . *(my, his)* 16

3 Verben

to be im present . . . . . *(I am, he is)* 19
to have im present . . . . . *(I have, he has)* 20
present progressive . . . . . *(I am speaking)* 21
simple present . . . . . *(I open, he opens)* 24
Gegenüberstellung: present progressive und simple present 28
going to-future . . . . . *(I'm going to buy)* 32
simple past . . . . . *(I opened, I was, I had, I went)* 33

4 Modalverben

can / can't / may / must 35

5 Satzarten

Fragesätze . . . . . *(Are they happy? Can he swim? Do they come?)* . . 37
Fragesätze mit Fragewort . *(When? Where? What? Why?)* 40
Subjektfragen . . . . . *(Who plays?)* 43
Verneinte Fragesätze . . . . . *(Haven't you got? Don't you know?)* 44

6 Wortstellung im Satz

Einfacher Aussagesatz . . . *(He plays football)* 46
Adverb der Häufigkeit . . . . *(often, always)* 47
Adverb der Zeit . . . . . *(every Friday)*, ... 48
Adverb des Ortes . . . . . *(in her room)* 48

TIPS TIPS TIPS T

Wir empfehlen dir, Übungen aus diesem Lernbereich auszuwählen, wenn du z.B. Schwierigkeiten mit dem Satzbau, den Zeiten, Fragesätzen oder Pronomen hast.

Wichtig ist, daß du möglichst bald loslegst, um die Lücken nicht zu groß werden zu lassen.

Um es dir einfacher zu machen, möchten wir dir vorschlagen, eine **Lernkartei mit Kärtchen** anzulegen. Informiere dich über die Lernkartei auf den Seiten 76 – 77. Auf die Karten schreibst du Beispiele zu einem grammatischen Merkstoff.

Und so könnten die Kärtchen aussehen:

	Vorderseite des Kärtchens	*Rückseite des Kärtchens*
	gehen **He / She**	go[1] **goes**[2]
oder:	essen ich esse **nicht** **er** ißt **nicht**	eat[1] I **don't** eat[2] he **doesn't** eat[2]
oder:	kommen **kommt er?**	come[1] **does he come?**[2]

Beim Abfragen überprüfst du nicht nur die Bedeutung und Schreibung des Wortes[1], sondern wiederholst auch grammatische Strukturen[2].

Zeichenerklärungen

Merksätze	Schwierig!	Achtung!	Vorsicht Falle!	Korrigiere die Fehler!	Übung im Heft

Fachausdrücke

Es ist ganz nützlich, wenn du diese Wörter auswendig lernst, weil sie wichtig sind, um grammatische Erklärungen zu verstehen. Das gilt für alle Sprachen!

Englisch	Deutsch	Beispiel
adjective	Adjektiv, Eigenschaftswort	old – alt expensive – teuer
adverb ~ of time ~ of place ~ of frequency	Adverb ~ der Zeit ~ des Ortes ~ der Häufigkeit	 on Saturday in London often, never
article	Artikel	a, an – ein, eine the – der, die, das
infinitive	Grundform Infinitiv	(to) be, (to) work, (to) think – sein, arbeiten, denken
modal verb	Modalverb	can – können must – müssen
noun	Substantiv, Hauptwort	girl – Mädchen house – Haus
personal pronoun	Personalpronomen, persönliches Fürwort	I, you, he – ich, du, er
possessive adjective	Possessivpronomen, (adjektivisch gebraucht) Besitzanzeigendes Fürwort	my, his – mein, sein
preposition	Präposition, Verhältniswort	at, in, on – an, in, auf
question word	Fragewort	who? – wer? when? – wann?
verb	Verb	to go – gehen

1 Artikel und Substantiv

1 Fill in 'a' or 'an'
Setze 'a' oder 'an' ein

a bike – *ein Fahrrad*   **an** old bike – *ein altes Fahrrad*

Du verwendest 'a' vor Wörtern, die mit einem Konsonanten (b, g, t, r usw.), 'an' vor Wörtern, die mit einem Vokal (a, e, i, o, u) beginnen.

an (h)our!! [aʊə]

a) A dog is . . an . . animal. It's . . a . . . small animal.

b) This is . . . . exercise-book. It's . . . . red one.

c) That is . . . . glass. It's . . . . . . empty glass.

d) Here is . . . . book. It's . . . . . . English book.

e) Tom is . . . . friendly boy. His brother is . . . . unfriendly person.

f) Mrs. Jones is . . . . young woman. Her mother is . . . . . . old lady.

g) This is . . . . boring story. I like . . . . interesting story.

h) Here is . . . . apple. There is . . . . banana.

i) I eat . . . . orange. It's . . . . sweet one.

j) . . . . lesson is forty-five minutes. . . . . hour is sixty minutes.

k) She is . . . . British girl. He is . . . . American boy.

l) Do you know . . . . answer to the question? It is . . . . . easy question.

Put into the plural. 2
Bilde den Plural.

a girl	→	two girl **s**	a box	→	two box **es**
a bag	→	some bag **s**	a lady	→	some lad **ies**
a house	→	two house **s**	a potato	→	lots of potato **es**

Den **Plural** bildest du, indem du **-s** anhängst.
Nach Zischlauten (x, s, sh, ch), nach Konsonant + y und oft nach -o schreibst du **-es**.

z.B. shelf – shelves

a) I can see fifteen ....girls..... (girl), sixteen ....boys........ (boy), two .... (baby) and three .... (lady) in the park.

b) There are lots of .... (cherry), ... (apple) and .... (peach) on the .... (shelf).

c) Diana has a lot of nice .... (dress) and .... (skirt), but she hasn't many .... (coat) and .... (shoe).

d) Mother has lots of .... (potato), twenty .... (egg), five .... (orange) and some .... (strawberry) in her bag.

e) How many .... (toy) has Jane got? – She's got two .... (doll) three yellow .... (ball) and two .... (plane).

f) I can see three .... (bus), five .... (van) and three .... (lorry) and two ....(taxi).

Die Rechtschreibung der Pluralwörter kannst du auf den Seiten 60-62 gründlich üben.

3 Give the plural of the words.
Bilde den Plural der Wörter.

Unregelmäßige Pluralformen: Die mußt du wohl oder übel auswendig lernen.

a mouse	–	ten	**mice**	a man	–	four	**men**
a child	–	two	**children**	a tooth	–	ten	**teeth**
a woman	–	three	**women**	a foot	–	two	**feet**

a) The Browns have two . . . . , Bill and Jane (child).

b) Mrs Brown and her sister are . . . . (woman).

c) Mr Brown and his father are . . . . (man).

d) Look! Two . . . . are watching the traffic (policeman).

e) Peter cleans his . . . . every morning and after dinner (tooth).

f) He washes his . . . . in the bath every day (foot).

4 Say it in English.
Sage es auf Englisch.

Überlege dir besonders die **Pluralformen:** Regelmäßige Bildung auf -s bzw.-es oder unregelmäßige Formen?

a) Sage, daß du 3 Äpfel, 5 Pfirsiche und viele Kirschen hast. → *I have ...*

b) Sage, daß vor dem Supermarkt 2 Autos, 3 Busse und 4 Lastwagen stehen.

c) Sage, daß die Kinder neue Kleider brauchen.

d) Sage, daß deine Mutter Kartoffeln, Äpfel, Orangen und Tomaten kaufen muß.

Singular and plural with this / these – that / those.
This / these bzw. that / those im Singular und Plural.

5

this apple	*dieser Apfel (hier)*	**these** apples	*diese Äpfel (hier)*
that apple	*dieser Apfel (dort)*	**those** apples	*diese Äpfel (dort)*

Singular	Plural	
this	**these**	dies hier: etwas Naheliegendes
that	**those**	dies dort, jenes: etwas weiter Entferntes

a) *This* . . . is an apple tree, . . *that* . . . tree over there is a cherry tree.

b) . . . . animals here are donkeys, ... animals over there are ponies.

c) . . . . girls over there come from another village,

. . . . girl here is Anne; she's from our school.

d) . . . . here are comics, ... over there is a magazine.

e) . . . . bird here is yellow, ... birds over there are green.

f) . . . . apples in my hand are red. . . . . apples on the trees are green.

Translate.
Übersetze.

6

a) Dieses Buch ist rot. → *This book is red.*
Welche Farbe hat das Buch dort?

b) Dies sind meine Bleistifte.
Die Bleistifte dort gehören Paul.

c) Das (hier) ist ein altes Haus.
Die Häuser dort in der Straße sind neu.

d) Sind das (dort) deine Freunde?
Ja. Es sind meine Freunde aus London.

e) Was ist das (hier)?
Es ist mein Fotoalbum.

7 Use the s-genitive: ('s) or (')?
s-Genitiv: ('s) oder (')?

Peter **'s**	family	– *Peters Familie*		the Potters **'**	house	– *das Haus der Potters*
the girl **'s**	bike	– *das Fahrrad des Mädchens*		the girls **'**	hats	– *die Hüte der Mädchen*
the men **'s**	hats	– *die Hüte der Männer*				

Bei Personen gebrauchst du den **s-Genitiv.** Er lautet **Apostroph + s** bei einem Wort im Singular (z.B. girl) bzw. einem Wort, dessen Plural nicht auf -s endet (z.B. men). Nach einem Plural -s (z.B. girls) schreibst du **nur Apostroph.**

a) The boy has a new shirt. *The boy's shirt is new.* ....

b) Jane has a green scarf. ....

c) The man has black shoes. ....

d) The Browns have friendly neighbours. ....

....

e) The girls have yellow hats. ....

f) The children have funny T-shirts. ....

....

g) The lady has a pretty dress. ....

h) The boys have blue trousers. ....

i) Our friends have a house in the country. ....

....

j) The women have red umbrellas. ....

....

8 Use the of-genitive.
Verwende den of-Genitiv.

the name	**of**	the street	–	*der Name der Straße*
the names	**of**	the streets	–	*die Namen der Straßen*

Bei Sachen nimmst du den **of-Genitiv.**

a) Our village has a very old church. The church has a red roof. → *The church of our village is very old. The roof of the church is red.*
b) England has a beautiful coast. London has very nice parks.
c) Our school has big rooms. This room has small windows.
d) Peter's car has blue seats. His car has black doors.
e) Our town has a new station. The train has a red locomotive.

9 Things you can buy.
Sachen, die du kaufen kannst.

a packet	of	cigarettes	–	*eine Schachtel Zigaretten*
two cups	of	coffee	–	*zwei Tassen Kaffee*

Zwischen der Mengenangabe und der Ware steht 'of'. Dieses 'of' wird im Deutschen nicht übersetzt.

cigarettes • milk • bread • jeans • sweets
potatoes • lemonade • tea • cake • toys

a) a packet of *cigarettes* ....
b) a slice of ....
c) a pair of ....
d) a cup of ....
e) a bag of ....
f) a piece of ....
g a box of ....
h) a glass of ....
i) a bottle of ....
j) a lot of ....

10 Translate.
Übersetze.

Welcher Genitiv ist richtig: **-s Genitiv** oder **of-Genitiv**?

a) Die Schule unseres Dorfes ist sehr klein. → *The school of our village is very small.*
Dort ist die Kirche unseres Dorfes.
b) Das hier sind die Bücher der Mädchen.
Wo ist das Fahrrad deines Bruders?
c) Ist Fußball das Hobby deines Freundes?
Der Name meines besten Freundes ist Robert.
d) Dover ist im Süden Englands.
Die Hauptstadt von Schottland ist Edinburgh.
e) Das ist nicht Herrn Browns Auto.
Die Straßen unseres Dorfes sind sehr schmal.
f) Kannst du mir ein Glas Milch bringen?
Geben Sie mir bitte ein Pfund Kartoffeln.
g) Das Haus meiner Tante ist am Ende der Straße.
Die Nummer des Hauses ist 20.
h) Das ist nicht das Haus meiner Eltern.
Das Haus meiner Eltern ist am Park.

11 Underline and correct the six mistakes.
Unterstreiche und verbessere die sechs Fehler.

a) The childrens are playing in the garden. ....*The children are playing*........
b) How many girl can you see over there? ....
c) The Millers shop is at the corner of the street. ....
d) This are apples from Italy. ....
e) Where can I get mens' hats? ....
f) My parent's house is near the river. ....

2 Pronomen und Mengenbezeichnungen

Fill in the missing words. 12
Setze die fehlenden Wörter ein.

	I	get up.	–	*ich stehe auf.*
Tom sees	**me.**		–	*Tom sieht mich.*
He helps	**me.**		–	*Er hilft mir.*
This is	**my**	book.	–	*Das ist mein Buch.*

Personalpronomen
(personal pronouns)

Possessivpronomen
(possessive adjectives)

als Subjekt			als Objekt					
I	*ich*	**wer oder was?**	me	*mich*	**wen oder was? wem?**	my	*mein*	**wessen?**
you	*du*		you	*dich*		your	*dein*	
he	*er*		him	*ihn, ihm*		his	*sein*	
she	*sie*		her	*sie*		her	*ihr*	
it	*es*		it	*es, ihm*		its	*sein*	
we	*wir*		us	*uns*		our	*unser*	
you	*ihr*		you	*euch*		your	*euer*	
they	*sie*		them	*sie, ihnen*		their	*ihr*	

a) *I* .... open *my* .... eyes. Can you see *me* .... ?

b) *You* .... open .... eyes. I can see *you* ....

c) .... opens .... eyes. I can see *him* ....

d) *She* .... opens .... eyes. Can you see .... ?

e) .... opens *its* .... eyes. We can see ....

f) .... open. .... eyes. Can you see ....

g) .... open .... eyes. We can see ....

h) *They* .... open .... eyes. We can see ....

13 Fill in the possessive adjectives.
Setze die Possessivpronomen ein.

Überlege, welche **Possessivpronomen** sinngemäß in die Lücken passen (Wem gehört es?). Beachte die englische Bezeichnung 'possessive adjectives'.

In the street:

a) Jean is walking along the street. She has a brown bag in . . . her . hand.

b) A car stops and Tom gets out. "Hallo, Tom", she says. "Is that . . . . . car?"

c) "Yes, it's . . . . car", he answers. "I saved up . . . . money and Dad is lending me some of . . . . money. "

d) "That's a lovely hat on . . . . head. Do you want a lift? I'm going to visit . . . . brother Jim. . . . . . . house is not far from the school."

e) "Thanks very much. I want to go to town to buy Sandra a present. It's . . . . birthday on Friday. . . . . parents are giving a big party."

f) "Yes, I know her. . . . . family live in the High Street."

g) "Do you know . . . . parents? They have got a shop."

h) "Yes, I do. I often go to . . . . shop to buy meat and sausages. "

i) Jean's brother Fred is coming along on . . . . bike.

j) "Hallo. Look, here is . . . . new bike. Where is . . . . . . bike, Tom?"

k) " . . . . bike's broken. This is . . . . brother's old bike. "

Fill in the missing personal pronouns or possessive adjectives. 14
Setze die fehlenden Personal- oder Possesivpronomen ein.

At school:

a) Peter: “You’ll have to stand, Alan. There is no chair for ....you..... .”

b) Alan: “Fine, ...I... will stand. That’s no problem for ....me...... .”

c) Anne: “Is this .... schoolbag, Mary?”

d) Mary: “No, ... must be Tom’s. ..... schoolbag is black, and this is grey.”

e) Alan: “There are lots of books on the desk. Can you see .... ?”

.... are blue and black and green. ”

f) Mary: “Where are Tom and Ian? Can you see .... ?”

g) Anne: “No, I can’t see .... can only see Mr Brown.

.... has a map in .... hand. Can you see ...... ?”

h) Alan: Oh, yes. .... know .... very well. .... teaches geography. We like Mr Brown, because ...... often tells ..... jokes.”

i) Peter: “Mr Brown is ..... form teacher. .... often goes for a walk with .... in .... free time.”

j) Anne: “Do .... know .... wife? .... is a very nice person, too. She sometimes invites .... to .... house.”

15 Say it in English.
Sage es auf Englisch.

Achte auf die Pronomen und die Wortstellung im Satz.

a) Sage, daß dein Fahrrad neu ist. "..........My bike is new.........."

b) Frage Tom, ob du sein Fahrrad haben kannst. "... ?"

c) Sage, daß Mary ihre Bücher unter dem Tisch hat. "..."

d) Sage, daß sie ihren Namen auf ihre Hefte schreiben muß. "... ."

e) Frage Mary, ob ihre Eltern in ihrem eigenen Haus wohnen. "... ?"

f) Sage, daß du ein neues T-Shirt hast und daß es rot ist. "... ."

16 Translate.
Übersetze .

a) Tom wäscht oft sein neues Auto.
Seine Schwester hilft ihm.

b) Sie waschen ihr Auto jede Woche.
Seine Farbe ist blau.

c) Dies ist unser Auto.
Es ist ein Rover.

d) Susan und Jill sind meine Schwestern.
Kannst du sie sehen?

e) Sie sind in ihrem Zimmer.
Ihr Zimmer ist nicht sehr groß.

f) Susan gibt Jill ihr Englischbuch und ihr Wörterheft.
Dann machen sie ihre Hausaufgaben.

3 Verben

Fill in: is – isn't – are – aren't. 17
Setze ein: is – isn't – are – aren't

Aussage	Kurzform	Verneinung	Kurzform	Frage
I am	I'm	I am not	I'm not	am I?
you are	you're	You are not	you aren't	are you?
he is	he's	he is not	he isn't	is he?
she is	she's	she is not	she isn't	is she?
it is	it's	it is not	it isn't	is it?
we are	we're	we are not	we aren't	are we?
you are	you're	you are not	you aren't	are you?
they are	they're	they are not	they aren't	are they?

Du übst die Formen (und Kurzformen) des Hilfsverbs **to be** – sein im **simple present**.

a) Geoff . .is. . from Macclesfield, but John and Paul (not) . . . . from Macclesfield. They . . . . from Manchester. Manchester . . . . a city in England.

b) . . . . . Sandra at school today? No, she . . . . . . at home because she . . . . ill. Geoff and Sandra . . . . her friends, but they (not) . . . . in the same class.

c) . . . . you English? – No, we . . . . English. We . . . . American.

d) . . . . . . you from France? – No, I . . . . from France. I . . . . from Germany.

Translate. 18
Übersetze.

a) Wieviel Uhr ist es, Tom? – Es ist 2 Uhr.
b) Bist du müde? – Nein, ich bin nicht müde.
c) Wo sind Bill und Mike? – Sie sind in der Schule.
d) Ist Susan auch in der Schule? – Nein, sie ist zu Hause.
e) Wie alt sind die Mädchen? – Susan ist 12, Anne ist 11.
f) Wie geht es den Mädchen? – Susan geht es gut, Anne ist krank.

Weitere Übungen zur Schreibung der Kurzformen findest du auf Seite 57.

19 Fill in: have – has.
Setze ein: have – has.

Aussage		Kurzform		Verneinung		Frage	
I have	got	I've	got	I haven't	got	have I	got?
you have	got	you've	got	you haven't	got	have you	got?
he has	got	he's	got	he hasn't	got	has he	got?
she has	got	she's	got	she hasn't	got	has she	got?
it has	got	it's	got	it hasn't	got	has it	got?
we have	got	we've	got	we haven't	got	have we	got?
you have	got	you've	got	you haven't	got	have you	got?
They have	got	they've	got	they haven't	got	have they	got?

Du übst die Formen (und Kurzformen) von **to have** – *haben* im **simple present**.
In der Umgangssprache nimmt man oft **'have got'**.

a) Bob . . . . two sisters, Sally and Gloria. They . . . . a black cat.

b) Their parents . . . . a big car. It . . . . red seats.

c) How many records . . . . you ? – I . . . . ten records.

d) Sally . . . . a doll, but she . . . . a ball.

e) We . . . . a new teacher. She . . . . black hair.

f) Jane . . . . very nice friends. They . . . . a lot of fun together.

20 Translate.
Übersetze.

a) Hast du einen Brieffreund?
Ja, ich habe einen Brieffreund in Amerika.

b) Hast du ein Fahrrad, Mike?
Ja, ich habe ein neues, schwarzes Fahrrad.

c) Hat deine Freundin ein eigenes Zimmer, Susan?
Nein, sie hat kein eigenes Zimmer.
Jill und ihre Schwester haben ein Zimmer zusammen.

d) Unsere Schule hat 500 Schüler.
Wieviele Schüler hat eure Schule, Jill?

Weitere Übungen zur Schreibung der Kurzformen findest du auf Seite 57.

Fill in the correct form of the verbs in the present progressive.
Setze die richtigen Verbformen im present progressive ein. **21**

I	**am**	speak**ing**	(I'm speaking)	*ich spreche (gerade)*
You	**are**	read**ing**	(You're reading)	*du liest (gerade)*
He	**is**	writ**ing**	(He's writing)	*er schreibt (gerade)*
We	**are**	sitt**ing**	(We're sitting)	*wir sitzen (gerade)*
They	**are**	wait**ing**	(They're waiting)	*sie warten (gerade)*

Du übst die Formen (und Kurzformen) des **present progressive** (= der Verlaufsform des Präsens). Eine solche Form gibt es im Deutschen nicht. Du nimmst eine Form von **to be** (- sein) und die **-ing Form** des Verbs.

Beachte die Schreibung, z.B. bei write → writing bzw. sit → sitting.

a) I ......am going...... (go) I'm ......going............

b) You .... (write) You ....

c) He .... (run) He ....

Tom .... (sit) He ....

d) She .... (read) She ....

Jane .... (eat) She ....

e) The dog .... (jump) It ....

f) We .... (come) We ....

g) You .... (wait) You ....

h) They...................... (play) They ....

The boys .... (swim) They ....

Vertiefende Übungen zur Rechtschreibung der -ing Formen (write → writing, sit → sitting) findest du auf den Seiten 63 und 64.

22 What are they doing?
Was machen sie gerade?

We	**are**	talking.	*Wir sprechen (gerade).*
We	**are not**	sleeping.	*Wir schlafen (gerade) nicht.*
	Are	you sleeping?	*Schlaft ihr (gerade)?*

Du übst auch die **Verneinung** und die Frage des **present progressive**. Die Formen sind einfach, weil du ein Hilfsverb hast (to be). Brauchst du eine Auffrischung, schau dir S. 19 noch einmal an.

a) Look, Bob 's doing .... his maths homework. *do*

He 's not listening .... to pop music. *not, listen*

b) ...... Peter .... to the radio? *listen*

No, he .... a letter to his penfriend. *write*

c) Why .... Judy .... the exercise? *not, do*

She .... her mother in the kitchen. *help*

d) Look, Mr. Stone .... out of the house. *come*

He .... shopping with his wife. *go*

e) Why .... the boys .... to school? *hurry*

They .... because they don't want to be late. *run*

f) Listen, Alan and Tony .... a terrible noise *make*

They .... the drums. *play*

Vertiefende Übungen zur Rechtschreibung der -ing Formen findest du auf den Seiten 63 und 64. Über die Kurzformen (he's, he's not, he isn't) kannst du dich auf Seite 57 informieren.

Say it in English. 23
Sage es auf Englisch.

Du verwendest beim Übersetzen **present progressive.** Die Verlaufsform beschreibt eine Handlung, die gerade stattfindet.

Was sagst du, wenn du jemand erzählst, daß

a) du gerade Geschirr abspülst, "I am washing up."

b) Tom gerade fernsieht, "....................................."

c) Susan gerade einen Brief schreibt, "....................................."

d) Peter gerade sein Zimmer aufräumt, "....................................."

e) Vater gerade das Auto repariert, "....................................."

f) dein Freund gerade seine Aufgaben macht. "....................................."

Was sagst du, wenn du jemand fragst,

g) was er gerade macht, "What are you doing?"

h) was er gerade liest, "....................................?"

i) wohin er gerade geht, "....................................?"

j) warum er gerade arbeitet, "....................................?"

k) wen er gerade anruft, "....................................?"

l) was er gerade ißt. "....................................?"

24 Put in the correct form of the verb. Use the simple present.

Setze die richtige Form des Verbs im einfachen Präsens ein.

I	open	–	*ich öffne*	→	I **don't** open	–	*ich öffne nicht*
you	open	–	*du öffnest*	→	you don't open	–	*du öffnest nicht*
he	opens	–	*er öffnet*	→	he **doesn't** open	–	*er öffnet nicht*
she	opens	–	*sie öffnet*	→	she doesn't open	–	*sie öffnet nicht*
it	opens	–	*es öffnet*	→	it doesn't open	–	*es öffnet nicht*
we	open	–	*wir öffnen*	→	we don't open	–	*wir öffnen nicht*
you	open	–	*ihr öffnet*	→	you don't open	–	*ihr öffnet nicht*
they	open	–	*sie öffnen*	→	they don't open	–	*sie öffnen nicht*

Du übst die Formen des **simple present** (= des einfachen Präsens). Die Verneinung bildest du mit **don't** bzw. **doesn't** und dem Verb in der Grundform.

Achte auf das -s in der 3. Person Singular (he / she / it / Tom / Mrs Moore opens).

a) I always .... early, but I ....
wake up — not, get up

b) You .... English, but you .... French.
speak — not, know

c) He .... a book, but he .... a newspaper.
read — not, read

d) She .... tea in the kitchen, but she .... it.
make — not, drink

e) It often .... here, but it .... very long.
rain — not, rain

f) We .... home for lunch, but we .... there.
go — not, stay

g) You often .... TV, but you .... to the cinema.
watch — not, go

h) They .... football every afternoon, but they ....
play — not, win

Übungen zur Rechtschreibung (he watches, she goes) findest du auf den Seiten 60-62.

Put in the correct form of the verbs. 25
Setze die richtige Form der Verben ein.

I open	*ich öffne*	→	**Do**	you open?	*Öffnest du?*
he opens	*er öffnet*	→	**Does**	he open?	*Öffnet er?*
she opens	*sie öffnet*	→	**Does**	she open?	*Öffnet sie?*
they open	*sie öffnen*	→	**Do**	they open?	*Öffnen sie?*

Die Frage beim **simple present** bildest du mit **do** bzw. **does** und dem Verb in der Grundform.

Does he open? Hier kommt kein -s in der 3. Person Singular, weil das -s bereits an die Form von to do (does) gehängt wurde.

a) What .... the children .... every morning? do

They .... into the bathroom and .... their teeth. go, clean.

b) .... father .... tea in the kitchen? make

Yes, he .... tea and .... breakfast. make, prepare

c) When .... school .... in the morning? start

School usually .... at half past eight. begin

d) What .... the children .... after school? do

They often .... football with their friends. play

e) Jenny never .... television in the afternoon. watch

She .... her homework when she .... home. do, come

f) What .... the children .... in the evening? do

They .... a book or .... to records. read, listen

Informiere dich über die Rechtschreibung (watch → watches, go → goes) auf den Seiten 60-61.
Fragesätze kannst du vertieft auf den Seiten 37-45 üben.

26 Say it in English.
Sage es auf Englisch.

Du verwendest beim Übersetzen **simple present**. Mit der einfachen Gegenwart drückst du aus, daß etwas **regelmäßig**, **oft** oder **gewohnheitsmäßig** geschieht.

a) Ich stehe jeden Tag um 6 Uhr auf. *I get up at six every day* ....

b) Um halb 8 verlasse ich das Haus. ....

....

c) Ich nehme immer den Bus. ....

d) Um 8 Uhr komme ich an der Schule an. ....

e) Ich mache nicht immer meine ....

Hausaufgabe. ....

f) Mein Freund hilft mir oft. ....

g) Nach der Schule spielen wir manchmal ....

Basketball. ....

h) Ich mag Basketball. ....

i) Einige meiner Freunde mögen es nicht. ....

....

j) Am Abend gehen wir oft ins Kino. ....

....

k) Mein großer Bruder fährt uns mit dem ....

Auto nach Hause. ....

l) Wir fahren jedes Jahr nach Schottland. ....

Dort besuchen wir meine Tante Jane. ....

Translate.
Übersetze.
27

Du übersetzt bejahte, verneinte und Fragesätze im **simple present.**

a) Patrick steht immer um 7 Uhr auf.
Er reinigt sein Zimmer jeden Tag.
Er geht oft zu Fuß zur Schule.
Manchmal fährt er mit dem Rad.

b) Rachel arbeitet in einem Supermarkt.
Am Sonntag arbeitet sie nicht.
Rachel spricht Englisch und versteht etwas Französisch.
Sie spricht nicht Deutsch.

c) Darren hat drei Schwestern und einen Bruder.
Sein Bruder hat viele Freunde.
Darrens Eltern wohnen in einem großen Haus.
Darrens Mutter arbeitet nicht.

d) Am Nachmittag macht Steven seine Hausaufgabe.
Dann trifft er seine Freunde.
Sie gehen oft in die Stadt.
Steven spielt nicht Fußball.

e) Liest James oft Bücher? – Nein.
Er mag Bücher nicht.
Warum sieht er oft fern?
Er mag interessante Filme.

f) Spielt Jenny ein Instrument?
Sie spielt Gitarre, aber sie spielt nicht oft.
Warum spielt sie nicht oft?
Sie hilft ihrer Mutter in der Küche.

g) Tony wäscht sich jeden Morgen.
Er putzt sich die Zähne und kämmt sich.
Er geht am Nachmittag auf den Spielplatz.
Er spielt aber nicht Fußball.

Übungen zur Wortstellung findest du auf den Seiten 46-50.

28 Say what these people are doing and how often they do it.
Sage, was die Leute machen, und wie oft sie es machen.

Are you drinking coffee, Susan? No, **I'm not drinking** coffee. **I drink** coffee every morning. **I'm drinking** tea. **I don't drink** it at night.

Halte die beiden Formen des **present** auseinander!
Present progressive: Etwas verläuft **gerade, eben, im Augenblick** (z.B. look, listen, just now, at the moment).
Simple present: Etwas geschieht **regelmäßig, oft, gewohnheitsmäßig** (z.B. every day, every week, every ... , often, always, usually).
Achte auf die verneinten Formen: I **am not** drinking – I **don't** drink.

a) Look. Jane .... in the river. swim
She .... every afternoon.

b) Look. Tom .... football . play
He .... football every Saturday.

c) Look. Mr Brown .... to a pub. go
He often .... to a pub with his friends.

d) Peter and his cousin .... to new records just now. listen
They .... to records every evening. not listen

e) Tom and Geoff .... computer games right now. play
They .... often .... together. not play

f) Look. Jennifer .... a show on TV. watch
She ....TV two or three times a week.

g) This is Martha. She .... shopping. go
She always .... shopping on Friday.

Present progressive or simple present?
Verlaufsform des Präsens oder einfaches Präsens?

29

Setze nun die richtige **Form des present** ein. Achte auf den Sinnzusammenhang und Signalwörter.

Bei einigen Verben (see, hear, know, hope, like und want) nimmst du nicht present progressive.

Dear Judy,

I . . . . (just / sit) . . . . at my desk. The sun . . . . (shine); it's a lovely day. I . . . . (write) to you because I . . . . (want) to thank you for your present. I . . . . (not / write) very often, I . . . . (not, be) very good at it. At the moment I . . . . (have) a cup of tea. I usually . . . . (have) tea in the afternoon. My brother . . . . (play) the guitar in the living-room; I can . . . . (hear) him. Jim and I often . . . . (play) football in the park. I . . . . (like, not) school. But just now I . . . . (enjoy) it. Our new geography teacher . . . . (be) very funny, and he sometimes . . . . (tell) us jokes. I must stop now. My sister . . . . (call). She always . . . . (call) me when she . . . . (want) to play with me. I . . . . (hope) to hear from you soon.

Lots of love,

George.

30 Say it in English.
Sage es auf Englisch.

Achte auf die richtige Zeit: **present progressive** oder **simple present.**
Du übst bejahte Sätze, verneinte Sätze und Fragen.

a) Du fragst Debbie, was sie **gerade** macht. “ .... ?”

Sie antwortet, daß sie ein Buch liest. “ ....”

b) Simon fragt dich, wohin du gehst. “ .... ?”

Du antwortest, du gehst **gerade** zum Supermarkt. “ ....”

c) Du fragst zwei Mädchen, was sie **gerade** machen und erfährst, daß sie einen Brief schreiben. “ .... ?”

“ ....”

d) Du fragst einen Mann, wann der Zug ankommt und erfährst, daß er **gewöhnlich um 8.30** ankommt. “ .... ?”

“ ....”

e) Simon sagt, daß er **jeden** Tag mit dem Rad zur Schule fährt, weil es nicht sehr weit ist. “ ....”

“ ....”

f) David sagt, daß er **oft** Tennis spielt, daß er aber nicht mit seiner Schwester spielt. “ ....”

“ ....”

Weitere Übungen zu Fragen findest du auf den Seiten 37-45.

Translate.
Übersetze.

31

Achte besonders auf die richtige Zeit – **present progressive** oder **simple present** – und auf die Wortstellung im Satz.

a) Tom: „Wo gehst du gerade hin, Mary?“
b) Mary: „Ich gehe ins Café.“

c) Tom: „Gehst du oft aus?“
d) Mary: „Ich treffe mich am Mittwoch immer mit meinen Freunden.“

e) Tom: „Schau. Dort kommt Jenny. Sie geht einkaufen.“
f) Mary: „Ich kaufe gewöhnlich am Samstag in der Stadt ein.“
g) Tom: „Ich helfe manchmal meiner Mutter. Mein Vater geht nie einkaufen. Er steht am Samstag gewöhnlich um 10 Uhr auf.“

h) Mary: „Ist deine Schwester zu Hause?“
i) Tom: „Nein, sie fährt gerade Fahrrad. Sie nimmt immer ihr Fahrrad, um zur Schule zu kommen.“

j) Mary: „Was macht dein Bruder gerade?“
k) Tom: „Er sitzt in seinem Zimmer und macht seine Hausaufgabe.“

l) Mary: „Macht er seine Hausaufgabe immer in seinem Zimmer?“
m) Tom: „Ja.“

Correct the six mistakes.
Verbessere die sechs Fehler.

32

a) Mary often <u>write</u> long letters. ...... writes ....

b) Look. Peter running to the tree. ....

c) Jane is listening to records every evening. ....

d) Tom and Billy goes home at ten o'clock. ....

e) The girls don't playing volleyball. ....

f) In the afternoon I do watch TV. ....

Weitere Übungen zur Wortstellung findest du auf den Seiten 46-50.

33 Use the correct form of 'be going to'.
Verwende die richtige Form von 'be going to'.

I **am going to** buy.	(I'm going to buy)	–	*Ich werde kaufen.*
He **is not going to** buy.	(He isn't going to buy)	–	*Er wird nicht kaufen.*
Are you **going to** buy?		–	*Wirst du kaufen?*

Du bildest das **going to-future** (= Futur mit 'going to') mit einer Form von **to be** + **going to** + dem **Infinitiv** des Verbs. Verneinung und Frage sind einfach, weil du sie mit 'to be' bildest. Erinnerst du dich noch? Wenn nicht, schlage nach auf Seite 19.

A birthday party:

a) Susan and David ..are going to have...... (have) a big birthday party next Saturday. They .... (invite) all their friends.

b) Bob .... (bring) a lot of new records. The children .... (not only, listen) to the music, but they .... (dance) all evening.

c) Mrs Stone .... (prepare) a lot of sandwiches, and Mr Stone .... (buy) fruit juice, lemonade and Coke.

d) Eric and Janet .... (have) a lot of fun at the party. Eric .... (eat) a lot because he is always hungry.

e) Jane .... (buy) beautiful flowers for Mrs Stone. She .... (not, buy) any sweets.

f) What (you, do) .... on your birthday? .... you .... (have) a party, too?

34 Complete the sentences. Use simple past.
Schreibe die Sätze zu Ende. Benutze das einfache 'past'.

I open.	– *Ich öffne.*	→ I open**ed.**	– *Ich öffnete.*
I don't open.	– *Ich öffne nicht.*	→ I **didn't** open.	– *Ich öffnete nicht.*
Does he open?	– *Öffnet er?*	→ **Did** he open?	– *Öffnete er?*

Du bildest das **simple past** (= die einfache Vergangenheit) von regelmäßigen Verben durch Anhängen von **-ed** an das Verb: open + **-ed** → opened. Frage und Verneinung bildest du mit did bzw. didn't und dem Infinitiv des Verbs.

Did he open_? Bei 'did' kommt kein -ed an das Verb, denn einmal 'past' (did) ist genug!

a) Where did the car **stop**? – It . . . stopped . . . . at the traffic lights.

b) When did the plane **land**? – It . . . . at quarter past two.

c) What did Paul **repair** last Friday ? – He . . . . his bike.

d) What did Anne **watch** last night ? – She . . . . a cowboy film.

e) Who did you **fetch** at the airport – I . . . . my cousin Hannes .

f) Did they **enjoy** their flight? – No, they . . . . it .

g) Where did Paul **stay** yesterday ? – He . . . . at home.

h) How long . . . . it . . . . yesterday? – It **rained** over five hours.

i) What . . . . Kevin . . . . last Saturday? – He **repaired** Jane's old bike.

j) Did John **help** his father yesterday? – No, he . . . . him.

Weiter Beispiele findest du auf den Seiten 63 und 64.

35 Put into the simple past.
Setze in das einfache 'past'.

I am	*ich bin*	I	**was**	*ich war*
we are	*wir sind*	we	**were**	*wir waren*
I have	*ich habe*	I	**had**	*ich hatte*
he has	*er hat*	he	**had**	*er hatte*
I go	*ich gehe*	I	**went**	*ich ging*
I speak	*ich spreche*	I	**spoke**	*ich sprach*
She speaks	*sie spricht*	She	**spoke**	*sie sprach*

Du übst das **simple past** von **unregelmäßigen Verben**. Diese Formen solltest du dir gut einprägen und auf deine Karteikärtchen übertragen (Siehe Seite 6!).

a) Today our teacher **is** very angry. Yesterday he ....*was*............... very friendly.

b) We **have** six lessons every day. Last Friday we only .... four lessons.

c) We often **do** our homework at school. Yesterday we .... it at home.

d) Tom usually **goes** to school by bike, but last week he .... by bus.

e) Jane often **reads** a story. Last Sunday she .... a newspaper.

f) The children usually **speak** English. In their last holidays they .... German.

g) Kirsty often **sees** grandmother in town. Yesterday she .... her in the supermarket.

h) Judy **takes** the dog for a walk. Last weekend she .... him to the park.

i) The train usually **leaves** at 11.30. Yesterday it .... at 11.45.

j) We **are** very good at maths. Last year we .... quite bad.

k) I **get up** at 7 o'clock every day, but yesterday I .... at 8 o'clock.

l) I often **eat** an ice-cream, but yesterday I .... some chocolates.

4 Modalverben: can, may, must

Say it in English. 36
Sage es auf Englisch.

Bob **can** swim, but he **can't** ride.	*Bob kann schwimmen, aber er kann nicht reiten.*
Can / **May** I have your bike?	*Kann / Darf ich dein Rad haben?*
Tom **must** help his father.	*Tom muß seinem Vater helfen.*

Can heißt können / dürfen. **May** heißt dürfen (besonders höflich). **Must** heißt müssen.

Du fragst einen Freund,

a) ob er dir helfen kann, "Can you help me ?"

b) ob du seinen Bleistift haben kannst, "................................ ?"

c) ob du sein Rad reparieren kannst, "................................ ?"

d) ob er zu Hause helfen muß, "................................ ?"

e) ob er am Nachmittag kommen darf. "................................ ?"

Er antwortet dir, daß

f) er nicht kommen kann, "................................ ."

g) er seiner Mutter helfen muß, "................................ ."

h) du mit seinem Bruder spielen kannst, "................................ ."

i) du um 4 Uhr kommen darfst, "................................ ."

j) sein Bruder nicht Volleyball spielen kann. "................................ ."

37 What do you say if...
Was sagst du, wenn...

Du verwendest **can** für können /dürfen und **may** für dürfen, wenn du besonders höflich sein willst.

a) ...du hinausgehen möchtest.

. . . .

b) ...du etwas auf deutsch erklärt haben möchtest.

. . . .

c) ...du das Rad deines Vaters nehmen möchtest.

. . . .

d) ...du etwas nicht beantworten kannst.

. . . .

e) ...du jemandem helfen möchtest.

. . . .

f) ...du nicht kommen kannst.

. . . .

38 Correct the four mistakes.
Verbessere die vier Fehler.

a) Tony cans swim in the ocean. . . . .

b) Sheila doesn't can ride a horse. . . . .

c) She can rides a bike. . . . .

d) Do we may watch television? . . . .

5 Satzarten

Ask questions. 39
Stelle Fragen.

They	**are**	happy.	*Sie sind froh.*	**Are**	they happy?	*Sind sie froh?*
He	**can**	swim.	*Er kann schwimmen.*	**Can**	he swim?	*Kann er schwimmen?*
We	**have (got)**	a ball.	*Wir haben einen Ball.*	**Have**	you (got) a ball ?	*Habt ihr einen Ball?*
Susan	**is**	sleeping.	*Susan schläft.*	**Is**	Susan sleeping?	*Schläft Susan?*
Bill	**was**	ill.	*Bill war krank.*	**Was**	Bill ill?	*War Bill krank?*

Du übst Fragesätze. Wenn im Aussagesatz ein Hilfsverb ist, z.B. eine Form von be (is, are, was), **can**, **must**, **have**, so stellst du dieses **Hilfsverb** im Fragesatz **vor das Subjekt**. Fragen, die du mit Ja bzw. Nein beantwortest, nennt man Entscheidungsfragen.

a) I am at home. – . . . . Is . . . . Tom at home?

e) We are tired. – . . . . you tired, too?

c) I have got a bike? – . . . . you . . . . a bike, too?

d) Jane is reading? – . . . . you . . . . , too?

e) I can swim. – . . . . you swim?

f) We must help in the kitchen?. – . . . . you help, too?

g) I am doing an exercise. – . . . . you doing an exercise,too?

h) I was in London. – . . . . you also in London last year?

Weitere Übungen zu Fragesätzen findest du auf den Seiten 22, 23 und 31 (present) sowie auf S. 33 (past).

40 Make questions.
Bilde Fragen.

They	come.	*Sie kommen.*	Do	they	come?	*Kommen sie?*
He	sits.	*Er sitzt.*	Does	he	sit?	*Sitzt er?*
Jane	answers	*Jane antwortet.*	Does	Jane	answer?	*Antwortet Jane?*
She	opened.	*Sie öffnete.*	**Did**	she	open?	*Öffnete sie?*

Wenn im Aussagesatz ein **Vollverb** steht, z.B. come, sit, answer, open (also kein Hilfsverb), setzt du im Fragesatz **do /does** (simple present) bzw. **did** (simple past) **vor das Subjekt**. Das Vollverb steht dabei im Infinitiv. Ein bloßes Umstellen (Kommen sie?) ist nicht möglich.

Does he sit_? Wenn du does verwendest, kommt an das Verb kein -s.

a) Tom eats an apple.

Does Tom eat an apple?

b) Geoff likes music.

c) The girls get up early.

d) Mr Brown drives to his office.

e) Mary and Jenny listen to pop records.

f) Father did all the housework yesterday.

Weitere Übungen zu Fragesätzen findest du auf den Seiten 22, 23 und 31 (present), sowie auf Seite 33 (past).

41 Say it in English.
Sage es auf Englisch.

Du bildest Fragen und überlegst: do / does oder Hilfsverb.

a) Frage Susan...

ob ihr Bruder zu Hause ist, "Is your brother at home ?"

ob sie Tennis spielen kann, " .... ?"

ob sie ein neues Fahrrad hat, " .... ?"

ob ihre Eltern in der Stadt sind. " .... ?"

b) Frage Bill,

ob er mit dem Rad zur Schule fährt, " .... ?"

ob er Rugby spielt, " .... ?"

ob er viel lernen muß, " .... ?"

ob er französisch sprechen kann. " .... ?"

42 Correct the six mistakes.
Verbessere die sechs Fehler.

a) Does the boy <u>eats</u> an apple? .... eat ....

b) Can Peter swimming? ....

c) Has Susan and her friend a new cap? ....

d) Must you helping in the kitchen? ....

e) Do Anne speak Italian? ....

f) Come you to town? ....

43 Ask for the underlined words. – Use question words.

Frage nach den unterstrichenen Wörtern. – Verwende Fragewörter.

Tom plays football	**in the garden.**	**Where**	does Tom play football?
They get up	**at eight.**	**When**	do they get up ?
Geoff is	**singing.**	**What**	is Geoff doing?
Tom must stay in bed	**because he is ill.**	**Why**	must Tom stay in bed?
Jane gets to work	**by train.**	**How**	does Jane get to work?

Du übst **Fragesätze mit Fragewörtern.** Das Fragewort steht am Satzanfang vor do/does/did oder einem Hilfsverb.

a) Geoff sits <u>in his living-room</u>.

. . . . ?

b) Bill gets up <u>at half past six</u>.

. . . . ?

c) The Browns get to work <u>by bus</u>.

. . . . ?

d) Mary often meets <u>her friend Sally</u>.

. . . . ?

e) Mr Brown drinks <u>a glass of beer</u>.

. . . . ?

f) Bill can't go to school <u>because he is ill</u>.

. . . . ?

g) Susan writes <u>a dictation</u>.

. . . . ?

h) They must be at the bus stop <u>at ten past seven</u>.

. . . . ?

Ask for the objects or other parts. 44
Frage nach dem Objekt oder nach anderen Teilen.

Du fragst nach dem Objekt mit **who(m)?** – wen? oder **what?** – was? – bzw. nach anderen Teilen mit **where? –** wo?, **when? –** wann?, **how long?** – wie lange? **why? –** warum?

a) The Browns live <u>near Manchester</u>.

Where do the Browns live .... ?

b) They have got <u>a nice flat</u> there.

.... ?

c) Mrs Brown likes <u>animals</u>.

.... ?

d) Jane goes to the judo club <u>every Thursday</u>.

.... ?

e) She meets <u>her friend Betty</u> there.

.... ?

f) Jane likes <u>music and dancing</u>.

.... ?

g) She often goes out on Saturday <u>because she wants to meet her friends</u>.

.... ?

h) Jane takes <u>her parents' car</u>.

.... ?

i) Mr Brown visited <u>his uncle</u> in New York last summer.

.... ?

j) He stayed in America <u>two weeks</u>.

.... ?

45 Say it in English.
Sage es auf Englisch.

Du übersetzt Fragesätze mit bzw. ohne Fragewort. Du achtest auf die verschiedenen Zeiten: a) und b) im simple present, c) im present progressive und d) im simple past.

a) Bill möchte wissen,

wann Barbara zur Schule geht, "When do you go to school ?"

wo sie wohnt, " . . . . ?"

ob sie mit dem Bus fährt. " . . . . ?"

b) Barbara fragt Bill,

wie alt er ist, " . . . . ?"

was er in den Ferien macht, " . . . . ?"

warum er in einem Laden arbeitet." " . . . . ?"

c) Barbara fragt Jane,

was sie gerade macht, " . . . . ?"

welches Buch sie gerade liest, " . . . . ?"

was ihr Bruder gerade macht. " . . . . ?"

d) Bill möchte wissen,

wann Jim nach London fuhr, " . . . . ?"

was er letzten Sonntag machte, " . . . . ?"

warum er nicht zur Party kam. " . . . . ?"

Fragesätze sind erfahrungsgemäß besonders schwierig. Du findest weitere Beispiele auch auf den Seiten 20-31 (simple present und present progressive) sowie 33-34 (simple past).

Ask for the subject. 46
Frage nach dem Subjekt.

S	
Peter	plays the guitar.
A cowboy film	comes next.
Tom's brother	helps us.
Five boys	play with us.
The yellow book	costs £ 10.

S		
Who	plays	the guitar?
What	comes	next?
Whose brother	helps	us?
How many boys	play with	us?
Which book	costs	£ 10?

Du fragst nach dem Subjekt mit **who?** – wer?, **what?** – was?, **whose?** – wessen? und anderen Fragewörtern.
Weil das Fragewort Subjekt des Satzes ist, brauchst du kein do/does oder did.

Nicht: Who play football? Sondern: Who plays football?

a) Jane goes to school at eight.

Who goes to school at eight .... ?

b) Jane's cousin plays cricket.

.... ?

c) Two of Jane's friends live in Manchester.

.... ?

d) The bike stands in front of the house.

.... ?

e) The boys get up at seven.

.... ?

f) Jessica got up at half past six.

.... ?

g) An accident happened.

.... ?

47 Form negative questions.
Bilde verneinte Fragen.

Have you got a bike?	→		**Haven't**	you got a bike?
Is he old enough?	→		**Isn't**	he old enough?
Do you get up early?	→		**Don't**	you get up early?
Who knows the answer?	→	Who	**doesn't**	know the answer?

Du übst verneinte Fragesätze. Bei Hilfsverben nimmst du **n't**, bei anderen Verben **don't** bzw. **doesn't**.

Beachte, daß du bei verneinten Subjektfragen doesn't nehmen mußt.

a) Are you from Scotland?

Aren't you from Scotland .... ?

b) Have you got a pen-friend in Italy?

.... ?

c) Do you read a book from time to time?

.... ?

d) What do you understand?

.... ?

e) Why does she sleep?

.... ?

f) Where can they park their car?

.... ?

g) Whose sister goes to the party?

.... ?

h) What fits into this bag?

.... ?

Translate. 48
Übersetze.

Du übersetzt Fragen mit bzw. ohne Hilfsverb. Es sind Fragen nach dem Objekt, anderen Teilen, dem Subjekt oder verneinte Fragen. Die Zeiten sind **present progressive** und **simple present**.

a) Was spielt ihr gerade?
Wohin gehen die Mädchen gerade?
Wer läuft gerade dort drüben?
Was macht Paul gerade?

b) Wann fährt der Zug ab?
Wo wohnen die Potters?
Warum spielt Jack Cricket?
Wie viele Bälle kauft Martin?

c) Wie alt ist Susan?
Wo können wir Tennis spielen?
Wann muß Peter seinem Vater helfen?
Wie teuer ist diese Schallplatte?

d) Wer spielt mit Barbara?
Wessen Schwester wohnt in der Stadt?
Wie viele Mädchen gehen zur Party?
Was hält vor der Schule an?

e) Wer spricht nicht Englisch?
Wer kommt nicht zur Geburtstagsfeier?
Wie viele Kinder gehen nicht zur Schule?
Warum hilft Peter uns nicht?

Correct six mistakes. 49
Verbessere sechs Fehler.

a) When <u>comes</u> Betty from school? When does Betty come from school?

b) Where does Patrick lives? . . . .

c) Where do you went last night? . . . .

d) How come you to school? . . . .

e) How many boys do play football? . . . .

f) Who does get up at six? . . . .

6 Wortstellung im Satz

50 Make sentences.
Bilde Sätze.

Subjekt	Verb	Object	
Geoff	plays	tennis.	*Geoff spielt Tennis.*
Susan	gets up	late.	*Susan steht spät auf.*
Subjekt	**Verb**	**andere Teile**	

Du übst die **Wortstellung** im einfachen Aussagesatz: Subjekt – Verb – Objekt bzw. Subjekt – Verb – andere Teile .

a) Geoff / the guitar / plays

Geoff plays the guitar ....

b) Jane / a picture / draws

....

c) Mr Brown / reads / the newspaper

....

d) The girls / a cake / bake

....

e) Tom / in the garden / plays

....

f) We / must / a dictation / write

....

Beachte den Unterschied zum Deutschen: Wir **müssen** ein Diktat **schreiben**.

Make sentences with adverbs of frequency. 51
Bilde Sätze mit Adverbien der Häufigkeit.

Geoff	**often**	plays tennis.	*Geoff spielt*	*oft*	*Tennis.*
Susan	**never**	gets up late.	*Susan steht*	*nie*	*spät auf.*
John can	**always**	stay.	*John kann*	*immer*	*bleiben.*
Bill is	**often**	late.	*Bill kommt*	*oft*	*zu spät.*

Das **Adverb der Häufigkeit** (– adverb of frequency) steht **vor dem Vollverb** (z.B. play, get up), **hinter dem Hilfsverb** (z.B. can) und **hinter** einer Form von **to be** (z.B. is).

a) Tom / eats / never / cornflakes

Tom never eats cornflakes

b) Jack / goes / always / before ten / to bed

c) The girls / go / usually / by bus / to school

d) Susan / often / must / help / her mother

e) James / often / is / ill

f) We / can / our car / always / park / here

g) The boys / played / often / football

Achte auf den Unterschied zum Deutschen!

52 Make sentences.
Bilde Sätze.

Geoff	goes	to the club	every Friday.	
Geoff	*geht*		*jeden Freitag*	*in den Club.*
			On Sunday	he visits his parents.
			Am Sonntag	*besucht er seine Eltern.*
Debbie	helps	her father	in the kitchen.	
Debbie	*hilft*	*ihrem Vater*	*in der Küche.*	

Das **Adverb der Zeit** (– adverb of time) steht meist am Anfang oder Ende des Satzes.
Das **Adverb des Ortes** (– adverb of place) steht meist am Satzende.

a) Peter / plays / football / every day

. . . .

b) Susan / goes / never / shopping / on Sunday

. . . .

c) Mr Brown / drives / at seven o'clock / to work

. . . .

d) They / visit / often / their parents / in Scotland

. . . .

e) The children / go to bed / usually / at ten o'clock

. . . .

f) Susan / every Friday / plays / the piano

. . . .

! Achte auf den Unterschied zum Deutschen!

Make sentences. 53
Bilde Sätze.

Debbie helps	her mother	**in the kitchen**	at the weekend.
Andy works		**in a supermarket**	on Saturday.
Debbie hilft	*ihrer Mutter*	*am Wochenende*	***in der Küche.***
Andy arbeitet		*am Samstag*	***in einem Supermarkt.***

Treffen ein Adverb des Ortes und ein Adverb der Zeit am Satzende zusammen, so steht Ort vor Zeit. Achte auf den Unterschied zum Deutschen!

a) Patrick/ in the garage / the car / washes on Fridays

. . . .

b) Stuart / in the living-room / in the evenings / television / watches

. . . .

c) Dawn / in the evening / plays / pop music / in her room

. . . .

d) James / on Saturdays / in the garden / football / plays

. . . .

e) The Potters / in summer / lots of flowers / have / in their garden

. . . .

f) Darren / often / to Wales / on holiday / goes

. . . .

g) Katie / to the swimming pool / goes / every Saturday

. . . .

h) Mr Robinson / shopping / goes/ on Monday/ at the supermarket

. . . .

54 Translate.
Übersetze.

Achte beim Übersetzen auf die richtige Stellung der **Adverbien des Ortes, der Zeit und der Häufigkeit.**

a) Ich fahre immer mit dem Bus zur Schule.
Am Samstag gehe ich nie zur Schule.
Am Sonntag gehe ich oft ins Kino.
Manchmal gehe ich am Nachmittag zum Schwimmen.

b) Tom sieht am Abend oft Fernsehen.
Am Samstag spielt er immer Fußball.
Tom ist immer freundlich.
In den Ferien liest er manchmal ein Buch.

c) Im Sommer arbeitet Mr Brown immer im Garten.
Am Sonntag geht er manchmal zum Fischen.
Die Browns gehen nie ins Kino.
Sie sitzen oft in ihrem Wohnzimmer.

d) Petra geht am Nachmittag oft spazieren.
Manchmal trifft sie Susan im Park.
Das Wetter ist im Sommer oft kalt.
Petra trägt im Winter immer einen Mantel.

e) Gestern sah ich einen Film im Fernsehen.
Ich habe letzte Woche oft ferngesehen.
Am Montag ging ich mit einem Freund in den Supermarkt. Wir kauften dort eine neue CD.

55 Find six mistakes and correct them.
Finde sechs Fehler und verbessere sie.

a) My sister draws often a picture. .... My sister often draws a picture .....

b) Our English teacher never is friendly. ....

c) I read always a morning paper. ....

d) We play every Tuesday in our club. ....

e) They go sometimes to the park. ....

f) He takes in the evenings his dog for a walk. ....

★ **Tips**
Lernkartei mit Hilfen für die Rechtschreibung 52

1 Besonderheiten
Große Anfangsbuchstaben .... *(English, Tuesday)* 53
Bindestrich .... *(twenty-one, twenty-first)* 55
Apostroph .... *(') (I've got, the boy's bag, the boys' bags)* .. 57

Lernzielkontrolle:
Übersetzung und Fehlerkorrektur 59

2 Schreibregeln
Endung -s oder -es .... *(caps, boxes)* 60
Endung -ys oder -ies .... *(boys, ponies)* 62
-e am Wortende fällt weg ...... *(come, coming)* 63
Konsonant verdoppeln .... *(get, getting)* 64

Lernzielkontrolle:
Übersetzung und Fehlerkorrektur 65

3 Schwierige Wörter
Wörter mit gleicher Aussprache . *(hour – our, know – no)* 67
Wörter mit stummen Lauten ... *(know, listen, comb)* 69

Lernzielkontrolle:
Fehlerkorrektur 70

4 Unterschiede zur deutschen Schreibweise
Leicht verwechselbare Wörter .. *(music – Musik, young – jung)* 71

Lernzielkontrolle:
Übersetzung und Fehlerkorrektur 73

Abschlußtest: Diktat 74

TIPS TIPS TIPS T

Übungen aus diesem Lernbereich solltest du bearbeiten, wenn du deine Rechtschreibkenntnisse systematisch verbessern möchtest. Wir empfehlen dir eine Erweiterung deiner Lernkartei. Sammle falsch geschriebene Wörter (aus dem Diktat, aus anderen schriftlichen Arbeiten) und übertrage sie auf die Kärtchen. Zum besseren Merken könntest du dir typische Fehlerquellen markieren, z.B.

	Vorderseite des Kärtchens	*Rückseite des Kärtchens*
	Kalender	**c**alend**a**r
oder:	45 fünfundvierzig	f**o**rty-five
oder:	schneiden + -ing	cu**t** cu**tt**ing

Die Rechtschreibung wird dir viel leichter fallen, wenn du gezielt wiederholst und dich auf schwierige Wörter, die du möglicherweise falsch schreiben würdest, einstellst.

Informiere dich über die Lernkartei auf den Seiten 76-77.

1 Besonderheiten

Fill in the correct words. 1
Setze die richtigen Wörter ein.

England	**E**ngland
an **E**nglish book	ein englisches Buch

Die Namen von Ländern und davon abgeleitete Wörter (z.B. Sprachen) schreibst du mit **großen Anfangsbuchstaben.**
Beachte den Unterschied zum Deutschen.

Countries...
Länder...

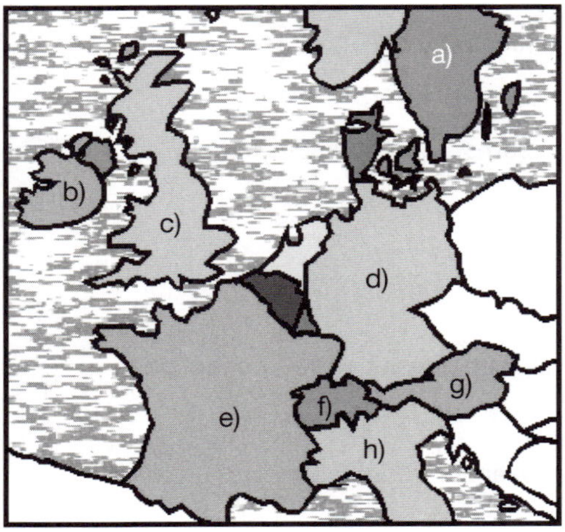

a) . . . .

b) . . . .

c) . . . .

d) . . . .

e) . . . .

f) . . . .

g) . . . .

h) . . . .

...and languages.
...und Sprachen.

i) In . . . . (b) they speak . . . .

j) In . . . . (e) they speak . . . .

k) In . . . . (d) they speak . . . .

l) In . . . . (g) they also speak . . . .

2 Put in the right letters.
Setze die richtigen Buchstaben ein.

school Schule

Im Gegensatz zum Deutschen schreibst du nicht alle Substantive mit großen Anfangsbuchstaben.

England, English
London, High Street, Big Ben
June, Monday, Christmas
winter, summer

Große Anfangsbuchstaben verwendest du nur am Satzanfang für das erste Wort, bei **I** – ich, für Länder und ihre Ableitungen, für Städte, Straßen und Gebäude, für Monate, Wochentage und Feste – nicht für Jahreszeiten.

Joan Collins:

Joan is an …nglish girl. She lives in …ondon, the …apital of …reat …ritain.

Joan's …ather is a …us …river, her …other is a …ousewife.

Joan goes to a …omprehensive …chool where she learns …nglish and …rench.

She doesn't learn any …erman.

Joan has lessons from …onday to …riday. Of course, she doesn't go to …chool on

…aturday and …unday. She is just preparing for her exam in …une . She has …ummer

…olidays in …ugust.

Joan has a …enfriend in …aris, and she wants to go to …rance in her …hristmas …olidays.

She has …riends in …cotland, and she sometimes visits them in the …utumn.

3 Write the full words.
Schreibe in ganzen Wörtern.

twenty-one	– *einundzwanzig*	twenty-first	– *(der) einundzwanzigste*
thirty-six	– *sechunddreißig*	thirty-sixth	– *(der) sechsundreißigste*

!!! Du übst die richtige Schreibweise der **Zahlen.** Beachte den **Bindestrich** zwischen Zehnern und Einerzahlen. Achte besonders auf:

four	fourteen	forty	fourth
five	fifteen	fifty	fifth
eight	eighteen	eighty	eighth

5	14	15	40
22	34	55	68

a) .... b) ....

c) .... d) ....

e) .... f) ....

g) .... h) ....

1.	2.	4.	5.
21.	32.	43.	54.

i) .... j) ....

k) .... l) ....

m) .... n) ....

o) .... p) ....

4 Make one word out of two.
Bilde ein neues Wort aus zwei Wörtern

apple-tree	*Apfelbaum*
textbook	*Lehrbuch*
stamp album	*Briefmarkenalbum*

Manche zusammengesetzte Wörter werden mit **Bindestrich** geschrieben, viele andere aber **zusammen** oder **auseinander**. Beachte die Unterschiede zum Deutschen.

looking • dining • **pen** • good
room • **friend** • pocket • record
money • player • pool • swimming

a) pen-friend or penfriend b) ....

c) .... d) ....

e) .... f) ....

grand • birth • **father** • work
day • post • home • card
shop • room • toy • bath

g) .... h) ....

i) .... j) ....

k) .... l) ....

shop • police • station • **assistant**
television • pet • set • orange
shop • juice • time • free

m) .... n) ....

o) .... p) ....

q) .... r) ....

Write the short form. 5
Schreibe die Kurzform.

I'm	**he's**	**we're**	**who' s**	**what's**	**it' s**	**can't**	**I' ve got**	**you' re not**
I am	he is	we are	who is	what is	it is	cannot	I have got	**you aren't**
	he has		who has					you are not

Du übst Kurzformen, die mit Apostroph geschrieben werden. Bei der Verneinung sind meist zwei Formen möglich, z.B. **you're not, you aren't.**

a)	**I am**	I'm	I am not	I'm not		
	you are	....	you are not	You're not	+	You aren't
	he is	....	he is not	....	+	....
	she is	....	she is not	....	+	....
	it is	....	it is not	....	+	....
	we are	....	we are not	....	+	....
	they are	....	they are not	....	+	....
b)	**I have got**	....	I have not got	....	+	....
	you have got	....	you have not got	....	+	....
	he has got	....	he has not got	....	+	....
	we have got	....	we have not got	....	+	....
	they have got	....	they have not got	....	+	....
c)	Here is	....	There is	....		
	That is	....				

d) What is this? .... this? Where is Bob? .... Bob?

Who is this? .... this? Who has got it? .... got it?

e) I cannot I .... I must not I. ....

6 Whose is it? Make sentences with the s-genitive.
Wem gehört es? Bilde Sätze mit dem s-Genitiv.

my sister**'s** bike the men**'s** hats the boy**s'** hats

Unterscheide zwischen der Endung 's und der Endung ' (nur Apostroph):
's als Genitiv bei Substantiven im Singular (sister) oder im Plural, der nicht auf -s endet (men); ' als Genitiv bei Substantiven im Plural mit Pluralendung -s (boys).

a) cousin My .... name is Oliver.

b) brother I can't find my .... exercise-book.

c) boy The .... cap is yellow.

d) girls These are the .... bikes. They are green.

e) Sandra Do you like .... new dress?

f) Mr Miller .... book shop is at the corner.

g) child This is a .... toy. Don't take it.

h) man The .... white shirt looks very nice.

i) woman A .... dress is often expensive.

j) children Can you show me the .... room?

k) lady Where can I buy a .... scarf?

e) parents Our .... house is small.

Weitere Übungen zum Genitiv mit ('s) bzw. (') findest du auf den Seiten 12 und 14.

Translate.
Übersetze.
7

Große Anfangsbuchstaben – Bindestrich – Apostroph.

a) Taschengeld ....
b) Großbritannien ....
c) Eßzimmer ....
d) Kinderabteilung ....
e) Jugendclub ....
f) Auskunftsschalter ....
g) Großvater ....
h) französisch ....
i) Polizeiwache ....
j) Herbst ....
k) Wolkenkratzer ....
l) Brieffreund ....

Correct the eight mistakes.
Verbessere die acht Rechtschreibfehler.
8

a) My french penfriend writes every Month.

....

b) Our Friend Brian lives in the Capital of England.

....

c) The Johnsons car is ten years' old.

....

d) They havent got a garage because its too expensive.

....

2 Schreibregeln

9 Add -s or -es.
Entscheide zwischen der Endung -s oder -es.

-s oder -es?

a girl	two girl**s**	a box	two box**es**
		a potato	some potato**es**
I speak	he speak**s**	I watch	she watch**es**
		I go	he go**es**

Auf **-s** endet der regelmäßige Plural von Substantiven (girls) bzw. die 3. Person Singular von Verben im simple present (he speaks, she comes, it puts); **-es** schreibst du in beiden Fälle **nach Zischlauten** (x, s, ss, sh, ch), bei manchen Substantiven auf -o * sowie bei den Verben **do** und **go**.

a) five (box) ....

b) three (glass) ....

c) two (bush) ....

d) some (dress) ....

e) ten (bike) ....

f) many (bus) ....

g) three (class) ....

h) some (pencil) ....

i) lots of (potato) ....

j) five (tomato) ....

k) Jane (get up) ....

l) He (watch) .... TV.

m) He (go) ....

n) She (wash) ....

o) He (fetch) ....

p) He (buy) .... it.

q) He (brush) ....

r) She (make) .... it.

s) Tom (do) .... it.

t) Jane (cross) .... the road.

* Aber: disco → discos, radio → radios.

Which is the correct ending: '-s , -es , ('s) or (')'? 10
Welche Endung ist richtig: '-s , -es , ('s) oder (')'?

-s oder -es?	book**s**	boxes
's oder s' ?	the boy**'s**	the boys**'**
's	he**'s** (he is / he has)	

Du mußt nun **mehrere Überlegungen** anstellen:
- Plural auf -s oder -es (→ Seite 60)
- Genitiv mit 's oder ' (→ Seite 58)
- Kurzformen (→ Seite 57).

a) The green book belongs to Tom, and the blue book belongs to him, too.

They are .... (Tom, book).

b) This hat belongs to Jane. It's a .... (girl, hat).

c) These .... (dress) are nice. They're ....

(women, dress).

d) These hats are for girls. They are .... (girl, hat).

e) This hat is for a man. It's a .... (man, hat).

f) These .... (glass) belong to Jane. They're .... (Jane, glass).

g) These .... (box) belong to the boys. They're the .... (boy, box).

h) .... (Geoff, is) from Manchester. ....

(Geoff, friend) are Michael and John.

i) The .... (Smith) live in Dartmoor. The .... (Smith) house

is in a lovely place.

j) .... (Who, is) this? – .... (It, is) Tom White.

k) .... (he, is) in .... (Jane) class.

l) .... (he, has) got lots of .... (cassette).

11 -ys or -ies?
-ys oder -ies?

y oder i?

a boy	two bo**ys**	a lorry	two lorr**ies**
I buy	she bu**ys**	I try	she tr**ies**

Auf **-ys** endet der Plural von Substantiven (boys) bzw. die 3. Person Singular von Verben im **simple present** (he buys, she plays, it plays); **-ies** schreibst du in beiden Fällen, wenn **vor dem -y** am Wortende ein **Konsonant** steht, z.B. try, hobby, pony.

a) five (family) ....
b) ten (day) ....
c) some (toy) ....
d) two (penny) ....
e) all my (hobby) ....
f) lots of (pony) ....
g) some (cherry) ....
h) two (key) ....
i) he (try) ....
j) she (buy) ....
k) he (play) ....
l) she (dry up) ....
m) she (carry) ....
n) he (worry) ....
o) he (hurry) ....
p) it (cry) ....

Weitere Übungen zum Plural findest du auf den Seiten 9-10, zum simple present auf den Seiten 23-26.

Fill in the -ing form. 12
Setze die -ing Form ein.

-e oder -? live — living, lived

Das stumme **-e** am Wortende der Verben **fällt** vor der **Endung -ing weg.** Du brauchst diese Formen zur Bildung des **present progressive**, z.B. He's living.
Das gleiche gilt vor der Endung -ed, wenn du die Formen des **simple past** bei regelmäßigen Verben bildest, z.B. live → lived.

a)	come	Who's . . . . ?
b)	dance	Sandra is . . . .
c)	use	I'm . . . . a sponge to clean the board.
d)	choose	What are they . . . . ?
e)	make	Peter is . . . . a kite.
f)	live	Where are you . . . . ?
g)	give	She's . . . . us an apple.
h)	change	The weather is . . . .
i)	prepare	Mother is . . . . breakfast in the kitchen.
j)	arrive	Look. The train from Liverpool is . . . .

Weitere Übungen zum present progressive findest du auf den Seiten 20-22,
zum simple past auf den Seiten 32-33.

13 Write the -ing form.
Schreibe die -ing Form.

Konsonant verdoppeln?	ge**t**	ge**tt**ing
	sto**p**	sto**pp**ed

Ein **Konsonant** am Ende eines Verbs **wird vor** der Endung **-ing verdoppelt**, wenn vor diesem Konsonanten ein einfacher Vokal ist, wie bei get → getting. Dies gilt also nicht bei wait → waiting, weil vor dem 't' zwei Vokale sind.
Die Verdoppelung gilt auch vor der Endung **-ed**, wenn du die Formen des simple past bei regelmäßigen Verben bildest, z.B. stop → stopped, aber nicht bei wait → waited.

a) get — Look. Little Tony is .... up.

b) stop — A car is .... at the traffic lights.

c) cut — Susan is .... some carrots.

d) run — Look. Peter is .... across the field.

e) wait — Why are you .... here?

f) hit — Jane is .... her head against the table.

g) sit — The girls are .... on the sofa.

h) bring — The milkman is just .... the milk.

i) put — Look. Jessica is .... her bike in the garage.

j) prepare — Jason is .... breakfast in the kitchen.

Weitere Übungen zum present progessive findest du auf den Seiten 21-23, zum simple past auf den Seiten 33-34.

14 **Translate.** *Übersetze.*

Beachte beim Übersetzen alle **Schreibregeln,** die du auf den Seiten 60-64 gelernt hast.

-s / -es?

a) Peter kauft 2 Bleistifte und 3 Hefte.
Er macht seine Hausaufgabe oft
am Nachmittag

b) Jane steht um 7 Uhr auf.
Sie wäscht sich und kämmt ihr Haar.
Sie fährt mit dem Rad zur Schule.

c) Frau White kauft Äpfel, Birnen,
Tomaten und Kartoffeln.
Sie holt alles im Supermarkt.

-ys / -ies ?

d) Paul hat viele Hobbys.
Er spielt oft mit seinen Spielsachen.
Er hat 2 kleine Lastwagen.

e) Mutter eilt zum Supermarkt.
Sie trägt eine große Tasche.
Sie kauft oft Kirschen und Orangen.

-e / - ?

f) Was macht Susan (gerade)?
Sie tanzt mit Paul.
Sie kommen näher.

g) Frau Potter deckt gerade den Tisch.
Die Potters essen gerade zu Mittag.
Martin nimmt eine Scheibe Brot.

Konsonanten verdoppeln ?

h) Schau. Tony läuft zum Haus.
Susan sitzt vor der Tür.
Sie wartet auf ihre Schwester.

i) Tony reparierte gestern sein Fahrrad.
Ein Auto hielt vor der Garage an.
Susan wartete an der Tür.

Achte auch auf die Wortstellung. Weitere Übungen findest du auf den Seiten 46-50.

15 Correct the mistakes.
Verbessere die Fehler.

Du kannst nun zeigen, ob du die vier allgemeinen Regeln zur Rechtschreibung beherrschst.

"Jennifer, what are you doing out there in the rain?"
"Geting wet!"

. . . .

"Lucy, do you know a girl called Emma Brown?"
"Yes, Mum. She sleepes next to me in geography class."

. . . .

Teacher: "Billy Clay, you're late again." Billy: "Sorry, sir. It's my bus – it's always comeing late."
Teacher: "Well, if it's late again tomorrow, catch an earlier one. "

. . . .

"Do you know why all the buses and trains are stoping today?"
"No, I don't. Why is that?"
"To let the passengers off."

. . . .

3 Schwierige Wörter

Choose the right words. 16
Wähle die richtigen Wörter aus.

Du übst **Homophone**. Das sind Wörter, die gleich ausgesprochen , aber verschieden geschrieben werden und eine andere Bedeutung haben. Halte sie auseinander!

there	**their**
sun	**son**
pair	**pear**
our	**hour**
meet	**meat**
too	**two**
right	**write**
see	**sea**
here	**hear**
know	**no**

a) The boys and ~ friends:

their ....

b) The ~ is shining:

....

c) It's a fruit:

....

d) It's sixty minutes:

....

e) You can eat it:

....

f) One and one is:

....

g) You can ~ with a pen.

....

h) I like to swim in it:

....

i) Can you ~ me?

....

j) Do you ~ the answer?

....

17 Fill in the correct word.
Setze das richtige Wort ein.

two	*zwei*	too	*auch*	to	*zu, um zu*
his	*sein*			he's	*er ist, er hat*
its	*sein*	it's	*es ist, es hat*		
there	*dort*	their	*ihr*	they're	*sie sind*
hear	*hören*	here	*hier*	her	*ihr*

Du übst Wörter, die **gleich oder ähnlich ausgesprochen** und deshalb häufig verwechselt werden. Beachte die unterschiedliche Bedeutung.

two – too – to a) The Browns have .... dogs, Patch and Bill. Mrs Black wants .... have a cat, ...

he's – his b) Tom cleans .... shoes every day, ... a very good boy, and all .... friends like him very much.

it's – its c) Where's the cat? –.......................... in the kitchen. .... lying on the sofa and drinking .... milk.

there – their – they're d) .... are fifteen boys in this class. .... good at football. .... trainer is very pleased.

her – hear – here e) Can you .... me, Tom? I'm on the roof. I can see the church from .... , and I can see Angela with .... nice red dress.

no – now – know f) Do you .... who this girl is? – I'm sorry I have .... idea. I must go home ....

18 Find the missing letter.
Finde die fehlenden Buchstaben.

k now
lis t en
com b

Du übst **Wörter mit stummen Lauten**. Du darfst Buchstaben, die nicht gesprochen werden, beim Schreiben nicht weglassen. Denke auch an Wörter mit einem stummen -e am Wortende, wie take, make. Übungen findest du auf Seite 63.

Welche Buchstaben sind am Wortanfang stumm?

a)	…ho	*wer*	d)	…our	*Stunde*
b)	…hose	*wessen*	e)	…nee	*Knie*
c)	…rong	*falsch*	f)	…rite	*schreiben*

Welche Buchstaben sind im Wort stumm?

g)	wa … k	*gehen*	k)	of … en	*oft*
h)	cu … board	*Schrank*	l)	ri … t	*richtig*
i)	ha … f	*halb*	m)	ta … k	*reden*
j)	dau …ter	*Tochter*	n)	w … en	*wann*

Welche Buchstaben sind am Wortende stumm?

o)	clim…	*klettern*	q)	autum…	*Herbst*
p)	com…	*Kamm*	r)	hi…	*hoch*

19 Write the words with the silent letter.
Schreibe die Wörter mit dem stummen Buchstaben.

a) talk milk walk ....

b) wrong write weather ....

c) climb lamp come ....

d) shelf half calf ....

e) how hour house ....

f) who water winter ....

g) knife knee know ....

h) often listen late ....

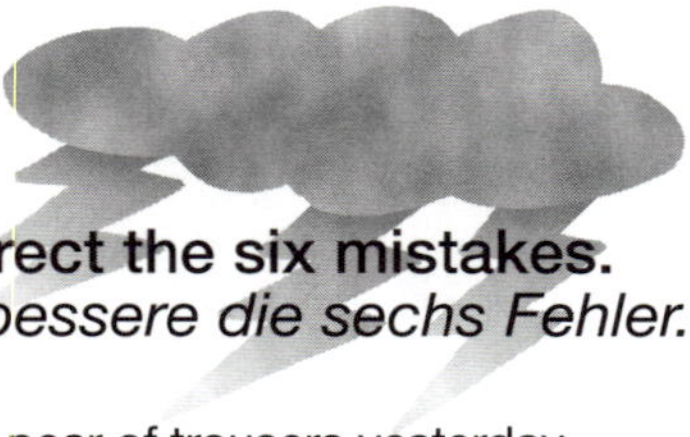

20 Correct the six mistakes.
Verbessere die sechs Fehler.

a) I bought a pear of trousers yesterday. ....

b) Their are some mistakes here. ....

c) It's nice when the son comes out. ....

d) Its cold in December. ....

e) Would you like to meat our son? ....

f) Autum is the season between summer and winter. ....

4 Unterschiede zur deutschen Schreibweise

Translate.
Übersetze. **21**

a) Adjektiv

b) Knie

c) Zucker

d) Salat

e) Marmelade

f) Sonntag

g) Idee

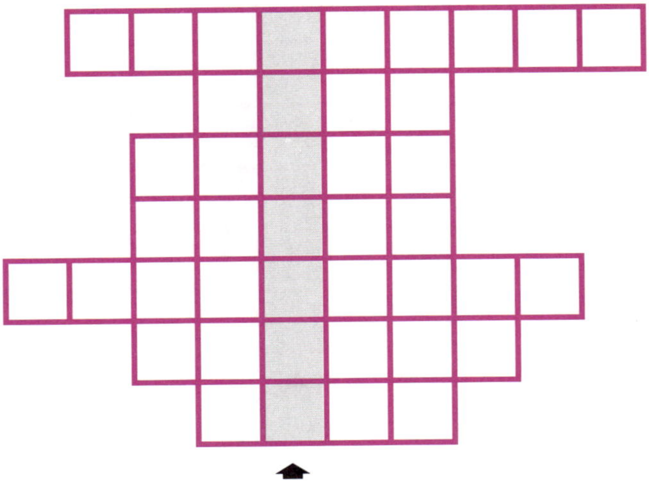

London is the capital of . . . .

h) Schuh

i) Dezember

j) Modell

k) Doktor

l) Telephon

m) Kappe

n) Onkel

o) Pudel

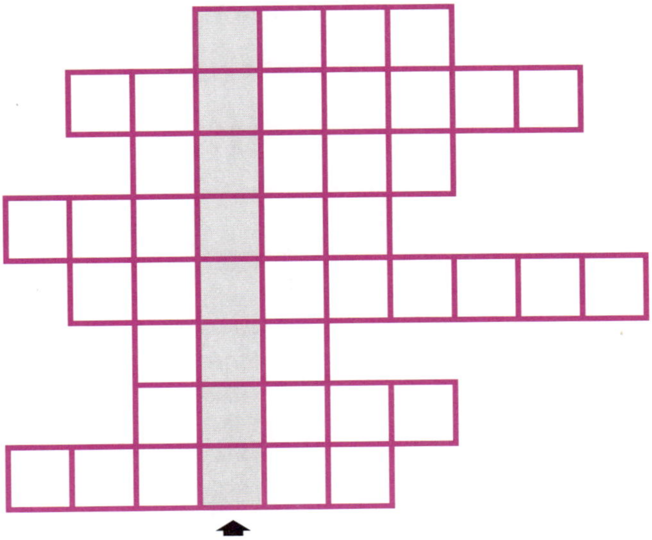

Edinburgh is the capital of . . . .

22 Translate.
Übersetze.

a) Musik

b) Gitarre

c) Objekt

d) Toilette

e) waschen

f) Kalender

g) Rekord

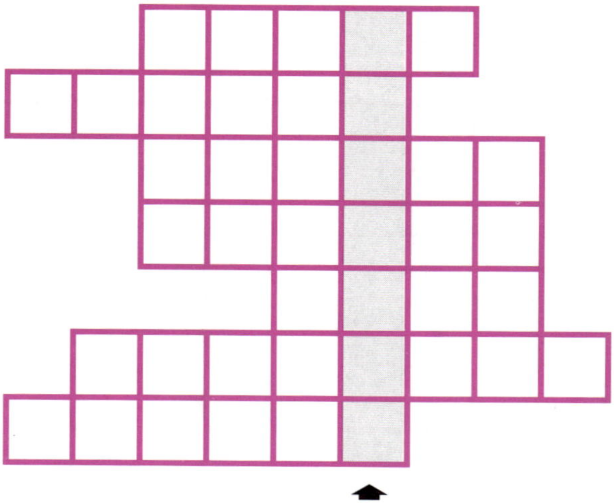

Dublin is the capital of . . . .

h) schwimmen

i) Limonade

j) Ambulanz (Krankenwagen)

k) Bier

l) Glas

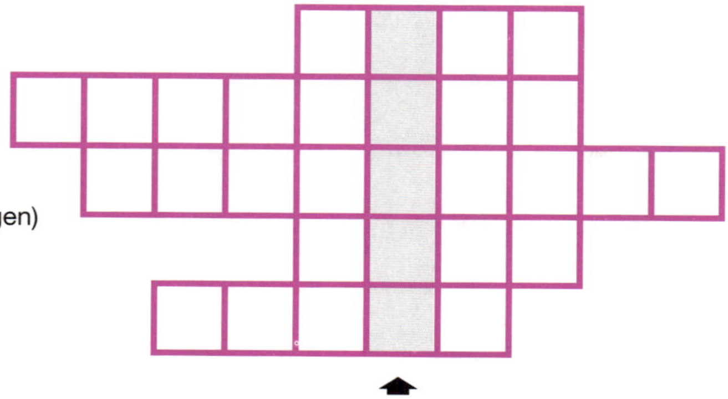

Cardiff is the capital of . . . .

23 Translate.
Übersetze.

apple	music	young	wash
Apfel	*Musik*	*jung*	*waschen*

Achte beim Übersetzen auf diese und auch andere Unterschiede zur deutschen Schreibung, auf Wörter wie *music*, *dictation*, *adjective*, *doctor*, *record*, d.h. *english* 'c' für deutsches 'k'.

a) Peters Geburtstag ist im Juli, Bettys im Oktober.
b) Zur Party gibt es Limonade, Bier und Kaffee.
c) Die spanischen Äpfel sind sehr gut.
d) England, Schottland, Wales und Nordirland sind das Vereinigte Königreich.
e) Herr Weiß spricht englisch. Er lebt in Amerika.
f) Sein Bruder ist Arzt in Kanada.
g) Das Fernsehprogramm ist nicht sehr gut.
h) Das Gras in unserem Garten ist hoch.
i) Kannst du den Dialog in einer Minute abschreiben?
j) Das Telefon läutet. – Es ist Onkel Paul.
k) Mein Onkel hat einen Pudel und eine Katze.
l) Patrick liebt Musik; er spielt oft Gitarre.

24 Correct the six mistakes.
Verbessere die sechs Fehler.

a) Pete always has marmelade on his toast. ....

b) Susan has to make a telephon call. ....

c) I would like a glass of limonade. ....

d) Miss Winter is a sekretary. ....

e) 'My' is a possessiv adjective. ....

f) This is an elektric train. ....

25 Dictation.
Diktat.

.... (Its, It's) your birthday soon, Alice," says Mrs Campell. "Do you want to have a party or are you .... (getting, geting) .... (too, two, to) old for that?" "I'll be .... (forteen, fourteen), mum," said Alice. "I'd like to invite a few .... (friend's, friends) to come bowling with me. Then maybe we could .... (sea, see) a film afterwards." "All right, but no more than three friends. This is .... (becomming, becoming) expensive," says Mr Campbell. "It was just as dear as eight years ago when Alice was six," said Mother. "Do you remember? We had Billy the Clown and I had to make all those .... (sandwichs, sandwiches) and cakes." "How could I forget?" .... (replys, replies) Mr Campbell. "I was covered from head to foot in ice .... (cream, kream) by the end and the dog was sick." "Well, you don't have to worry about that this year, dad," says Alice and she .... (goes, gos) up to her room to .... (right, write) to three of her friends and invite them to her birthday party.

Du könnest dir – wenn du nicht allein übst – das ganze Diktat auch diktieren lassen. Einige schwierige Wörter sind enthalten: bowling – Kegeln, expensive – teuer, dear – teuer, covered – bedeckt, you don't have to worry – du mußt dir keine Sorgen machen.

⋆ Tips

Lernkartei mit Vokabelkärtchen 76

1 Wörter sammeln und ordnen

Körperteile – Kleidung 78
Fahrzeuge – Möbel 79
Getränke – Speisen – Tiere 80
hören *(hear, listen to)* – sehen *(see, look)* – sprechen *(speak, talk, tell)* 81
machen *(do, make)* – tragen *(carry, wear)* 82
Verben und Substantive zuordnen *(to clean the board)* 83

2 Wörter einsprachig erklären

Einfache Defintionen 84
Gegensätze *(opposites)* – Adjektive *(early – late)* 85
Gegensätze *(opposites)* – Substantive *(brother – sister)* 86
Gegensätze *(opposites)* – Präpositionen *(behind – in front of)* 86
Gegensätze *(opposites)* – Verben *(sit-stand)* 87

3 Wörter richtig anwenden

„Falsche Freunde“ ...... *(Who – wer, where – wo)* 88
„Kleine Wörter“ .... *(but, only, still, always)* 89
Präpositionen der Zeit ... *(at ten, on Monday, in 1995)* 91
Uhrzeit angeben 92
Präpositionen
des Ortes .... *(at, on, in)* 93
Präpositionen
der Richtung........... *(into, to, out of; across)* 94
Präpositionen
im übertragenen Sinn 95
Etwas aussagen,
über etwas berichten 96
Einfache Interviews 97

TIPS TIPS TIPS T

Die Übungen auf den folgenden Seiten helfen dir, englische Wörter besser zu behalten und auch selbst anzuwenden.

Außerdem schlagen wir dir vor, eine **Lernkartei mit Vokabelkärtchen** anzulegen. Die Kärtchen hierfür könnten so aussehen:

	Vorderseite des Kärtchens	*Rückseite des Kärtchens*
oder:	Brief	letter
oder:	schreiben	to write
	früh	early

Die Vokabeln und ihre deutsche Bedeutung sammelst du im Unterricht, entnimmst sie den Wörterlisten deines Schulbuchs oder überträgst sie aus den folgenden Übungen dieser Lernhilfe. Du könntest einen Teil deiner Kärtchen mit zusätzlichen Informationen zur Grammatik oder Rechtschreibung erweitern. Dies kannst du auf den Seiten 6 für die Grammatik und 52 für die Rechtschreibung nachlesen.

LERNKARTEI:

Deine Lernkartei besteht aus einem Kasten mit 5 Fächern.
Die Größe der Kärtchen hängt von der Größe des Kastens ab.

Wir empfehlen dir folgende Übungsschritte:

1. Schreibe neue Vokabeln auf Kärtchen – englisch auf die Vorderseite und deutsch auf die Rückseite.

2. Lerne beide Seiten des Kärtchens auswendig. Du kannst dabei herumlaufen, du mußt nicht ruhig am Tisch sitzen!

3. Sage das englische Wort nicht nur laut, sondern schreibe es zur Kontrolle noch einmal auf einen Zettel.

4. Beherrschst du ein Wort sicher, legst du das Kärtchen in Fach 2.

5. Von Zeit zu Zeit (z.B. jede Woche) wiederholst du früher abgefragte Vokabeln. Du beginnst mit den Kärtchen im Fach 2 und überprüfst dein Wissen. Kannst du ein Wort immer noch sicher, so wandert das Kärtchen in Fach 3, hast du es aber vergessen, so wandert dieses Kärtchen in Fach 1 zurück.

6. Nach diesem Muster des Aufsteigens und Absteigens läuft das 'Spiel' bis Fach 5.

1 Wörter sammeln und ordnen

1 Find the words.
Finde die Wörter.

Du sammelst Wörter zu den Oberbegriffen: **Körperteile (parts of the body) und Kleidung (clothes)**. Dabei erweiterst du auf praktische Weise deinen aktiven Wortschatz.

Parts of the body
Give the English words.

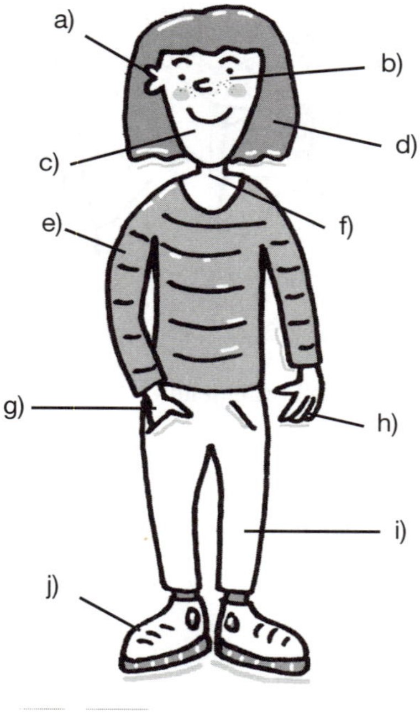

a) . . . . b) . . . .

c) . . . . d) . . . .

e) . . . . f) . . . .

g) . . . . h) . . . .

i) . . . . j) . . . .

Clothes
Translate.

k) Hut . . . . l) Hemd . . . .

m) Hosen . . . . n) eine Hose . . . .

o) ein Paar Jeans . . . . p) Bluse . . . .

q) Mantel . . . . r) Kleid . . . .

s) Rock . . . . t) Strumpfhose . . . .

u) Schuhe . . . . v) Socken . . . .

Find the words. 2
Finde die Wörter.

Du sammelst Wörter aus den Bereichen **Fahrzeuge** (vehicles) und **Möbel** (furniture).

Vehicles:
Give the English words.

a) ....

b) ....

c) ....

d) ....

e) ....

f) ....

g) ....

h) ....

Furniture:
Translate.

i) Stuhl ....

j) Sessel ....

k) Tisch ....

l) Schreibpult ....

m) Schrank ....

n) Regal ....

o) Bett ....

p) Uhr ....

q) Fernseher ....

r) Radio ....

s) Bild ....

t) Kamin ....

3 Find six words for each group.
Finde sechs Wörter für jede Gruppe.

Du sammelst Wörter aus den Bereichen **Tiere, Speisen** und **Getränke.**

beer • bread • bird • budgie • cake • cat • cheese • coffee • dog • egg • horse • lemonade • marmalade • milk • mouse • orange juice • salad • tea

a) **Tiere** (animals)

....

....

b) **Speisen** (food)

....

....

c) **Getränke** (drinks)

....

....

4 Fill in the correct words.
Setze die richtigen Wörter ein.

hören	to hear	*hören*	to listen to	*anhören, zuhören*
sehen	to see	*sehen*	to look at	*anschauen*
			to look for	*suchen*
sprechen	to say	*sagen*	to tell	*erzählen*
	to talk	*reden*	to speak	*sprechen*
	to ask	*fragen*	to answer	*antworten*

Du übst Wörter zu den Oberbegriffen „hören“, „sehen“ und „sprechen“.
Achte auf die Unterschiede!

hear – listen

a) Ian can .... the dog in the garden. He's barking.

b) The radio is on. Rachel is .... to music.

c) Can you .... what Lucy is saying?

see – look

d) What can you .... in the picture? I can .... a cat.

e) .... at the picture and tell me if you like it.

f) Mary is .... for her umbrella. It's raining.

answer (2x) **– ask – say – speak – talk – tell**

g) Tom .... me : “Where are you going, Peter?”

h) I .... : “I'm going to the youth club.”

i) Tom .... : “That's great. .... me, what are you doing there?”

j) I .... : “I want to .... to Barbara.”

5 Decide between these verbs.
Entscheide dich zwischen diesen Verben.

machen	to do	*tun*	to make	*machen, herstellen*
tragen	to wear	*tragen, anhaben*	to carry	*tragen, befördern*

Du übst Wörter zu den Oberbegriffen „machen“ und „tragen“.
Beachte auch hier die unterschiedliche Bedeutung.

do – make

a) What does you mother .... ? – She's a secretary.

b) What are you .... here? – I'm .... a cake.

c) Let's .... this exercise again, boys. It is not very good.

Don't .... the same mistakes again, please.

d) Five apples and three bananas! – That .... £ 2, please.

e) What is Geoff .... in the garden? – He's .... a model plane.

carry – wear

f) Mary is .... a red skirt today. She often ....skirts.

g) Peter must help his mother. They are .... a big box.

h) When Mr Ward goes out, he always .... a blue coat.

i) Boys often .... lots of things around with them in their pockets.

j) The magician often .... a red hat and a dirty old coat.

Achte auch auf die richtigen Endungen, z.B. she wear**s**, she is wear**ing**.

Find a suitable noun. 6
Finde ein passendes Substantiv.

Du ordnest Substantive bestimmten Verben **zu**, die sinngemäß gut zusammenpassen.

board • bike • dishes • door • flowers • game
homework • newspaper • photo • trousers • TV • tree

a) to clean the board ....
b) to climb ....
c) to do ....
d) to open ....
e) to pick ....
f) to play ....
g) to read ....
h) to ride ....
i) to take ....
j) to wash ....
k) to watch ....
l) to wear ....

Which noun belongs to which verb? 7
Welches Substantiv gehört zu welchem Verb?

a) to ask
b) to listen to
c) to fill in
d) to clear
e) to dry
f) to spend
g) to wait for
h) to draw
i) to write
j) to throw

1) money
2) the bus
3) the table
4) the dishes
5) a letter
6) music
7) a picture
8) a ball
9) a question
10) a word

Nehmt Stifte unterschiedlicher Farbe, damit das "Spinnennetz" übersichtlicher wird.

Wenn du in vollständigen Sätzen üben möchtest, findest du Aufgaben zum Satzbau auf den Seiten 46-47.

2 Wörter einsprachig erklären

8 **Find the correct words.**
Finde die richtigen Wörter.

Du erklärst Wörter, indem du einfache Sätze zu Ende schreibst.

bathroom • **bedroom** • cinema
dining-room • living-room • playing-field
bus stop • instrument • satchel • kitchen

a) You sleep in the . . . bedroom . . . .
b) You wash in the . . . .
c) You listen to the radio and watch TV in the . . . .
d) You eat in the . . . .
e) You play football on a . . . .
f) You wait for the bus at the . . . .
g) You put your books and exercise-books in the. . . . .
h) Mother cooks in the . . . .
i) You watch a film in the . . . .
j) A guitar is a nice . . . .

Später wirst du die Wörter ohne Hilfestellung erklären können.

Find the opposites.
Finde das Gegenteil. 9

Is it **cold**? No, it's **warm**.

Du erklärst Wörter einsprachig, indem du ein **opposite** findest. Ein **opposite** ist das Gegenteil zu einem Wort, z.B. cold – kalt – warm – warm.

black • clean • early
full • good • left
long • noisy • right ←
old • slow • small

bad • big • dirty
empty • late • quick
quiet • new • right ←
short • **white** • wrong

a) black ≠ white

b) .... ≠ ....

c) .... ≠ ....

d) .... ≠ ....

e) .... ≠ ....

f) .... ≠ ....

g) .... ≠ ....

h) .... ≠ ....

i) .... ≠ ....

j) .... ≠ ....

k) .... ≠ ....

l) .... ≠ ....

10 Put in the feminine form.
Setze die weibliche Form ein.

Du erklärst Verwandtschaftsbezeichnungen durch ein **opposite**.

a) brother .... b) boy ....

c) son .... d) husband ....

e) man .... f) father ....

g) uncle .... h) grandmother ....

11 Fill in opposites.
Setze das Gegenteil ein.

Du erklärst die Bedeutung von **Präpositionen** durch ein **opposite**.

past • without • to
under • outside • out of
in front of • downstairs

a) Is Tom behind the house? No, he's ..in front of.................... it.

b) Does Kathy go into the kitchen? No, she comes .... it.

c) Is it five to ten? No, it's five .... ten.

d) Are the girls upstairs? No, they're ....

e) Do you go with your parents? No, I want to go .... them.

f) Is Jill coming from school? No, she is going .... school.

g) Is the budgie inside the cage? No, it's................................. .

h) Is the picture over the couch? No, it's .... it.

12 Use opposites.
Verwende das 'opposite'.

School **starts** at 8 o'clock. Lessons **end** at three o'clock.

Du erklärst Verben, indem du ein opposite findest. Achte auf die richtige Form deines Lösungswortes, damit es sinngemäß in die Satzlücke paßt, z.B. school starts (it starts) – aber: lessons end (they end).

answer • arrive • buy • come out • end • get up
hate • put on • save • sit • sit down • shut

a)	Tom is standing at the window.	Jane is .... on a chair.
b)	Don't stand up, girls.	.... , please.
c)	Jim is opening the window.	Jill is .... it again.
d)	School starts at 8 o'clock.	Lessons .... at 1 o'clock.
e)	I go to bed at 9 o'clock.	I must .... at 6 o'clock.
f)	Jack takes off his coat.	The other boys .... their coats.
g)	I often spend a lot of money.	My sister.............................. most of it.
h)	Mr Black sells his car.	Mr White wants to .... a new car.
i)	Geoff likes football and hockey.	But he .... squash.
j)	Paul is going into the classroom.	The girls are .... of the room.
k)	The teacher asks a question.	Who can .... it ?
l)	The train arrives at 9.25.	It .... at 9.32.

3 Wörter richtig anwenden

13 Fill in: who – where – why – because.
Setze 'who, where, why' oder 'because' ein.

who	heißt	*wer*
where	heißt	*wo*
why	heißt	*warum*
because	heißt	*weil.*

Halte diese häufig gebrauchten Wörter auseinander. Man bezeichnet sie als „falsche Freunde".

a) .... is at the door? – It's Tom.

b) .... is Mary? – I think she is still at school.

c) .... are you going to the youth club? – I must talk to Barbara.

d) The boys are happy .... they have no homework to do.

e) .... must Daddy wash his car? – It's so dirty.

f) Can you tell me .... Peter is? – He's in the kitchen.

g) .... can answer my question? – Barbara. She knows everything.

h) .... can't Geoff come and play football with us?.

– He must stay indoors .... he is ill.

i) John's brother doesn't know .... has stolen his bike.

j) Mr Potter asked me .... the station is.

Fragesätze kannst du auch auf den Seiten 40-45 üben.

Which word fits best? 14
Welches Wort paßt am besten?

again – *wieder, noch einmal*		**altogether** – *insgesamt*	
always – *immer*		**but** – *aber*	
every – *jeder*		**many** – *viele*	
much – *viel*		**of course** – *natürlich*	
only – *nur*		**sometimes** – *manchmal*	
still – *(immer) noch*		**too** – *auch*	

Du übst „kleine Wörter", die immer wieder vorkommen und die oft falsch angewendet werden. Präge dir die Bedeutung deshalb genau ein.

a) It's very late in the evening, and I'm .... doing my homework.

b) I like pop music, and my friend Barbara likes it, ...

c) £100 is too .... money for a child. Isn't it?

d) I never get up late; I .... get up early.

e) This exercise is not very good; I must do it ....

f) Can you speak English? – Yes, ... I am from England.

g) How .... girls are there in this room ? – Twenty, I think.

h) How much is all this? – It's £50 ....

i) I don't often play tennis, and I .... play badminton.

j) .... morning Peter must get up at seven o' clock.

k) I like soccer and tennis, ... I don't like rugby.

l) There are .... four lessons on Monday; our maths teacher is ill.

15 Say it in English.
Sage es auf Englisch.

Achte beim Übersetzen besonders auf „falsche Freunde“ und „kleine Wörter“.

Frage...

a) wer Englisch sprechen kann, “ .... ?”

b) wo der Spielplatz ist, “ .... ?”

c) warum Susan nach Hause geht, “ .... ?”

d) wieviel das Buch kostet, “ .... ?”

e) wieviele Freunde Tom hat. “ .... ?”

Sage, ...

f) daß du immer früh aufstehst, “ ....”

g) daß du manchmal schwimmen gehst, “ ....”

h) daß du jeden Tag liest, “ ....”

i) daß du nur zwei Bücher hast, “ ....”

j) daß deine Eltern immer noch “ ....
in London sind. ....”

Übungen zu Fragesätzen findest du auf den Seiten 40-45, zur Wortstellung auf Seite 47.

When is it? Fill in: 'in – on – at'. 16
Wann ist es? Setze 'in – on – at' ein.

Du übst Präpositionen der Zeit. Du nimmst **at** bei der Uhrzeit und bei Festen, **on** bei Tagen und **in** bei Monaten, Jahren, Jahreszeiten und Tageszeiten.
in the morning, in the afternoon, in the evening – aber: at night

a) .... 1995 b) .... spring c) .... Christmas

d) .... 8 o' clock e) .... July f) .... Monday

Translate. 17
Übersetze.

a) Frau Potter geht am Samstag immer einkaufen.
Sie steht um 7 Uhr auf.

b) Judys Geburtstag ist im Mai.
Sie gibt am 12. Mai eine große Geburtstagsparty.

c) Patrick spielt im Winter Eishockey und im Sommer Fußball.
Die Spiele sind oft am Samstag.

d) Am Morgen gehen Susan und ihr Bruder zur Schule.
Am Nachmittag machen sie ihre Hausaufgaben.

e) Toms Geburtstag ist an einem Sonntag.
Seine Freunde treffen sich schon am Samstag um 20 Uhr.

18 What time is it?
Wie spät ist es?

Du gibst die Uhrzeit an. Die erste halbe Stunde rechnest du von der vorhergehenden Stunde an mit **past** = nach (z.B. two minutes past, five past, a quarter past, half past), danach rechnest du auf die nachfolgende Stunde hin mit **to** = vor (z.B. twenty to, a quarter to, three minutes to).

a) .... ten   b) a quarter ....   c) .... seven

d) a quarter ....   e) .... eight   f) ..... minutes ..... eight

19 Translate.
Übersetze.

a) Judy steht um halb sieben Uhr auf.
Um Viertel vor acht geht sie zur Bushaltestelle.

b) Der Bus fährt drei Minuten vor acht ab.
Die erste Stunde beginnt zwanzig Minuten nach acht.

c) Die Schule endet um halb drei.
Judy ist zehn vor drei zu Hause.

d) Der Film beginnt um Viertel nach acht.
Judy trifft ihre Freunde um fünf vor acht vor dem Kino.

Weitere Übungen zur Stellung der Zeitadverbien findest du auf den Seiten 48-50.

Fill in: at – in – on. 20
Setze 'at, in' oder 'on' ein.

at	the bus stop	**in**	the house	**on**	the roof
at	the cinema	**in**	the middle	**on**	the wall
at	school	**in**	the picture	**on**	the left
at	*an, in*	**in**	*in, auf*	**on**	*auf, an*

Du übst **Präpositionen des Ortes.** Du fragst **Wo**?

a) Susan and her friends are . . . . the youth club. It is . . . . the town.

b) John is swimming . . . . the river. His sister is . . . . school.

c) Tony is lying . . . . the lawn. Jane is waiting . . . . the corner.

d) Jane is not at home, she is . . . . the doctor's. She's sitting . . . . a chair.

e) . . . . the picture you can see a horse . . . . the left and a tree . . . . the right.

f) Jane is sitting . . . . the table. There is a vase . . . . it.

Say it in English. 21
Sage es auf Englisch.

Sage, daß…

a) der Tee in der Tasse ist.
b) die Tasse auf der Untertasse ist.
c) die Tasse auf dem Tisch ist.
d) Martin nicht zu Hause ist.
e) er in der Schule ist.
f) die Spielsachen im Schrank sind.
g) das Buch auf dem Fußboden liegt.

22 Fill in: into – to – out of – across.
Setze 'into, to, out of' oder 'across' ein.

I go	**into**	the house
I go	**to**	school
I come	**out of**	the room
I run	**across**	the street

Du übst Präpositionen der Richtung. Du fragst: Wohin? bzw. Woher?

a) It's raining; Susan is running . . . . the house to get an umbrella.

b) Martin is looking . . . . the window. Can you see him?

c) Jack has got a flu, he must go . . . . the doctor.

d) He goes . . . . the house and goes . . . . the bus stop.

e) He gets . . . . the bus when he sees the doctor's house on the other side.

f) He walks . . . . the road and goes . . . . the house.

23 Translate.
Übersetze.

a) Simon geht oft ins Kino.
b) Am Samstag geht Rachel in die Disco.
c) Schau. Tom rennt über die Straße.
d) Peter fährt immer mit dem Rad zur Schule.
e) Schau. Susan geht gerade aus dem Zimmer.
f) Peter wirft gerade den Ball über den Fluß.
g) Mary übersetzt den Text gerade ins Französische.
h) Ich trinke gerade Tee aus einer roten Tasse.
i) Wir fahren oft nach England.
j) Die Mädchen gehen gerade in ihr Zimmer.

Übungen zur Wortstellung findest du auf den Seiten 47-50.

Fill in: at – by – in – into – of – on – out of – to. *Setze ein: 'at – by – in – into – of – on – out of – to'.* 24

Du übst Präpositionen der Zeit, des Ortes und der Richtung und auch Präpositionen mit anderen Bedeutungen (by – of).

to go	**by**	train	–	*mit dem Zug fahren*
to go	**by**	car	–	*mit dem Auto fahren*
to go	**by**	bus	–	*mit dem Bus fahren*
a packet	**of**	cornflakes	–	*ein Packet Cornflakes*
a lot	**of**	people	–	*viele Leute*

Merke dir besonders: to go by car / bus / train = mit dem Auto / Bus / Zug fahren

a) There are a lot ...... people .... the street. Some are waiting ...... the bus stop. They want to go .... bus, they are not going .... train.

b) Two ladies are looking .... a shop window. .... the left they can see shoes and .... the right there are a lot .... beautiful dresses.

c) A young man with lots .... things is coming .... supermarket. He is carrying them .... his car. The car is .... the car park.

d) Some girls are .... their way .... school. They must be .... school .... five minutes. The first lesson starts .... half past eight.

e) Tom is not .... home, he is already .... school. He goes .... his classroom and takes his exercise-books .... his schoolbag.

f) .... the weekends Tom is often .... his uncle's .... the country. When his uncle visits the town he stays .... a hotel .... Baker Street.

g) Tom's aunt is .... hospital. Her husband visits her every day .... the afternoon. Aunt Kate wants to be home again .... Christmas.

25 What do they say in English?
Wie heißt es auf Englisch?

Du machst Angaben zu **dir selbst**. Oft kannst du nicht Wort für Wort übersetzen, z.B. Ich **habe** Glück – I **am** lucky.

a) Ich habe Glück.
b) Es tut mir leid.
c) Ich habe Hunger.
d) Es ist schade.
e) Ich brauche nicht zu kommen.
f) Ich komme zu spät.
g) Mir geht es gut.
h) Ich muß zu Hause bleiben.
i) Ich habe Durst.
j) Ich bin froh.

1) I'm hungry.
2) I'm late.
3) I needn't come.
4) I'm lucky.
5) I'm thirsty.
6) I'm happy.
7) I'm sorry.
8) It's a pity.
9) I'm all right.
10) I must stay at home.

Wenn du verschiedenfarbige Stifte nimmst, siehst du besser, welche Sätze zusammengehören.

26 Fill in: There is – there are.
Setze 'there is' bzw. 'there are' ein.

There is	a vase on the table.	*Auf dem Tisch steht eine Vase.*
There are	ten boys in the room.	*Im Zimmer befinden sich zehn Buben.*

Du berichtest über **Personen oder Sachen** mit **there is** (+ Wort im Singular) bzw. **there are** (+ Wort im Plural). Die deutsche Übersetzung ist meist etwas freier.

a) .... a picture on the wall. It shows a horse.

b) In this room .... twenty-five children.

c) How many boys .... on the playingfield?

d) .... over twenty boys there, I think.

e) But .... only one boy from my class.

f) .... two American pupils in my class.

Choose the correct answer. 27
Wähle die richtige Antwort aus.

Hallo, I'm Jane.

What's your name?

Du beantwortest einfache Fragen als Vorübung zu einem **Interview**.

twelve • Monday • Scotland
1st April • half past ten • cornflakes
£5 • it's fine • brown
Billy • boys • I've got a flu.

a) What's your name? ..Billy..........................
b) How old are you? ....
c) Where do you come from? ....
d) What day is it today? ....
e) What's the date today? ....
f) What's the time? ....
g) What's the weather like? ....
h) What's for breakfast? ....
i) How much is this bag? ....
j) What colour is your bag? ....
k) How many are you? ....
l) What's wrong with you? ....

28 Translate.
Übersetze.

Du übst einfache Fragen, die für eine Unterhaltung ganz nützlich sind.

a) Wo kommst du her?
Bist du Engländerin oder Amerikanerin?
Wie alt bist du?
Was sind deine Hobbys?
Hast du Geschwister?

b) Wie spät ist es?
Wie geht es dir?
Wie geht es deinen Eltern?
Wie heißt dein neuer Lehrer?
Wann stehst du am Morgen auf?

c) Hast du ein Fahrrad?
Habt ihr einen Garten zu Hause?
Haben deine Eltern ein oder zwei Autos?
Hast du einen Brieffreund?
Gehst du oft auf Partys?

29 Say it in English.
Sage es auf Englisch.

a) Du begrüßt deinen Freund Simon am Morgen und fragst, wie es ihm geht.

b) Du begrüßt Herrn Moore am Nachmittag und sagst ihm, daß deine Eltern leider nicht zu Hause sind.

c) Du begrüßt Alan und fragst ihn, ob er mit ins Kino geht. Alan antwortet, daß er leider keine Zeit hat. Er muß seiner Mutter helfen.

d) Du fragst Emma, ob sie zu deiner Geburtstagsfeier kommen kann. Emma sagt natürlich Ja.

Übungen zu Fragen findest du auf den Seiten 37-45.

★ **Tips**
Vorbereitung auf schriftliche Arbeiten 100

	Grammatik	Rechtschreibung	Wortschatz	
1. Test				101
	this/that – these/those	-ing Form	Farben	
	Plural	's	Getränke	
	present progressive	Zahlen	Fahrzeuge	
	to be, to have			
2. Test				104
	possessive adjectives	-ing Form	Wörter einsetzen	
	Fragesätze	Homophone	Interview	
	may/must/can	Jahreszeiten	Zahlen	
3. Test				107
	simple present	Wochentage	Interview	
	present progressive	-s / -es	Über etwas berichten	
	Fragesätze	Homophone		
	must			
4. Test				110
	possessive adjectives	-s	Präpositionen (Zeit)	
	simple present	-ing Form		
	present progressive	Homophone		
	Wortstellung			
5. Test				113
	simple present	-s / -es	Farben	
	Fragesätze		nach Zeit, Preis und	
	verneinte Aussagesätze		Aussehen fragen	
	Genitiv			
6. Test				116
	Wortstellung im Satz	's	Präpositionen (Ort)	
	Fragesätze	-ing Form	Interview	
	verneinte Aussagesätze		falsche Freunde	
7. Test				119
	Personalpronomen	-s Genitiv	Worterklärungen	
	possessive adjective	-s / -es		
	going to-future	Homophone		
8. Test				122
	Fragesätze	s-Genitiv	opposites	
	verneinte Aussagesätze	-s / -es		
	Wortstellung	Bindestrich		
	past tense			

TIPS TIPS TIPS

Die folgenden Tests helfen dir bei der Vorbereitung auf alle schriftliche Arbeiten.

★ Bearbeite die Tests, wenn sie **vom Stoff her** zu dem **passen**, was du im Unterricht gerade durchnimmst. Sie sind so zusammengestellt, daß die Inhalte der Grammatik ähnlich wie in den meisten Lehrwerken aufeinander folgen.

★ In jedem Falle solltest du auch hier **deine persönlichen Schwerpunkte** setzen. Auf der vorhergehenden Seite kannst du den Stoff der einzelnen Tests nachschlagen. Übrigens: Auch bei den Diktaten mußt du zeigen, daß du in Grammatik und Wortschatz fit bist.

★ Schreibe deine Antworten in die Lücken oder freien Zeilen bzw. in ein Übungsheft und **vergleiche** sie dann mit den Lösungsvorschlägen.

★ **Kreuze deine Fehler** deutlich **an** und bearbeite die Aufgaben noch einmal, und zwar so oft, bis du wirklich zufrieden sein kannst.

★ Betrachte die Tests als eine Art von **Prüfungstraining**:

– Du siehst, wie eine schriftliche Arbeit in der Schule aussehen könnte.

– Du kannst dich auf eine Arbeitszeit von etwa 45 Minuten einstellen.

– Du gewinnst Routine und bist dann im „Ernstfall" viel sicherer.

★ Du kannst die Tests als „krönenden" Abschluß deiner Arbeit an bestimmten Kapiteln auffassen, aber auch – ohne große Vorbereitung – einsteigen, um zu sehen, wie gut du schon bist.

Viel Erfolg!

1. Test

Dictation. 1

Emma Potter is twelve years old. She's got a sister and a brother. Her sister's name is Katie and her brother's name is David. Katie is fifteen and David is only nine.

They've got three pets: a dog Toby, a cat Pussy and a budgie. They live in a nice house with a large garden. In the garden there are fruit trees and lovely flowers.

Emma's parents are very nice. The family has got a small car – a Mini.

At the moment Mrs Potter, Emma's mother is cooking the dinner and Mr Potter is reading his newspaper. David is repairing his bike and Emma is helping him.

Write in words. 2

a) 25 – 15 = 10

. . . .

b) 5 + 9 = 14

. . . .

c) 13 + 4 = 17

. . . .

d) 55 – 19 = 36

. . . .

e) 42 + 56 = 98

. . . .

f) 55 – 15 = 40

. . . .

3 Put in this, that, these, those, pair(s).

a) Mrs Potter: How much are .... skirts over there?

Assistant: They're twenty-three pounds ninety-five.

b) Emma: And how much is .... dress here?

Assistant: It's forty-two pounds fifty.

c) Mrs Potter: How much is .... altogether?

Assistant: .... makes sixty-six pounds forty-five.

d) Mrs Potter: What are .... over there?

Assistant: They are four .... of blue jeans.

e) Emma: Look, there are two .... of white shorts

on .... shelf there.

Mrs Potter: Yes, they are lovely.

f) Emma: Mum, can I have a .... of .... jeans here?

Mrs Potter: Yes, can you see .... jeans in the window there?

I think we'll take a .... of them.

Find more words. 4

a) The children drink milk for breakfast.
Name four other drinks:

. . . . , ... , ... , ...

b) A car is a vehicle.
Name four other vehicles:

. . . . , ... , ... , ...

c) Father gets a yellow tie for his birthday.
Name four other colours:

. . . . , ... , ... , ...

Put into the plural. 5

a) The man is waiting for the bus.

. . . .

b) The car is in the garage.

. . . .

c) The woman is riding a bike.

. . . .

d) The child has an orange.

. . . .

e) The boy is eating a cake.

. . . .

f) The lorry is in the street.

. . . .

2. Test

1 Dictation.

It's Saturday afternoon. The sun is shining and the Potters are at home.

Mr Potter is working in the garden and Mrs Potter is busy, too. She is cleaning the windows. Katie is helping her mother. At three o'clock her friend Lucy is on the phone. "I'm going to the swimming-pool. Are you coming?" "Yes, I am," Katie answers, "I'm just getting my bike."

Now Katie and Lucy are lying in the sun. They've got a cassette-recorder and they are listening to a new cassette and they are talking about their next holidays.

A young woman is watching the two girls. It's Mrs Moore, their German teacher.

2 Fill in.

The calendar:

a) There are .... days

and .... weeks in a year.

b) March is the .... month of the year, ... is the

sixth month and May is the .... month.

c) The four .... are: ...., summer,

.... and ....

d) When is your birthday? – It's on ....

....

Fill in the possessive adjectives. 3

a) The Potters and .... bikes:

b) Mr Potter has got a very old bike. .... paint is coming off and David is painting .... father's bike in the garage.

c) Mrs Potter is in the garage, too. She has got to repair.......................... bike because it has got a puncture. But she can't find .... repair kit.

d) "Where is .... repair kit, David? Have you got it?". – . "No, I haven't got .... repair kit. Isn't it in .... bag?"

e) Now David is cleaning .... mother's bike. Mrs Potter is very pleased because all .... bikes are OK.

f) Mrs Potter:" .... bikes are fantastic now." On Sunday the Potters can go to Easton Park on..................... 'new' bikes.

Find the correct words (play, do, talk to, watch, repair). 4

a) You .... your friends on the phone.

b) You .... a film on TV.

c) You .... your bike when it has got a puncture.

d) You .... your homework in the afternoon.

e) You .... music on a cassette-recorder.

5 Translate.

Katie Potter hat Tiere gern. Sie möchte Mr Davenport in seiner Tierhandlung helfen.
So geht sie in sein Geschäft.

a) Katie grüßt Mr Davenport und	Katie: " ....
fragt, ob sie die Tiere in seinem	....
Geschäft anschauen darf.	....?"
b) Mr Davenport erlaubt das	Mr D.: " ....
natürlich. Er fragt Katie, ob sie	....
ein Haustier hat.	....?"
c) Katie verneint es. Ihre Eltern haben	Katie: " ....
nur eine kleine Wohnung, und sie	....
haben keinen Garten.	....?"
d) Sie fragt Mr Davenport, ob sie	" ....
ihm am Nachmittag helfen kann.	....?"
e) Sie sagt ihren Namen, und daß	" ....
sie 12 Jahre alt und Schülerin	....
an der Park School ist.	....?"
f) Mr Davenport antwortet, daß sie	Mr D.: " ....
die Tiere füttern und säubern muß.	....
Er fragt, ob sie jeden Donnerstag	....
nachmittag um 3 Uhr kommen	....
kann.	....?"
g) Katie bejaht. Aber sie muß ihre	Katie: " ....
Mutter fragen.	....?

3. Test

Dictation. 1

Simon Moore is a disc jockey. That's a very interesting job. You can meet him at the disco in Brynton Road every Friday, Saturday and Sunday afternoon.

The programme starts at four o'clock, but Simon must leave home at half past two. He goes to the disco in his car. He arrives there at three o'clock. His records and cassettes are in a big brown box. He carries them to his record player. Of course there are lots of pop stars in his programme. All the boys and girls listen to them because they are their favourite singers.

You can have drinks or eat cakes, biscuits and sandwiches there. Simon finishes work at ten o'clock. He is tired and soon goes to bed.

Fill in the pronouns. 2

Katie's party.

a) Katie : "Hallo, Rachel and Jenny, come in. It's nice to see . . . ."

b) Rachel: "Hi, Katie, happy birthday!"

c) Jenny : "Look, I've got something for . . . ."

d) Katie : "Oh, is that for . . . . ?"

e) Jenny : "Yes, of course. Open . . . ."

f) Rachel: "Where are David and Darren? I can't see . . . ."

g) Katie : "The boys are in the garden. They are waiting for . . . ."

"I can see . . . . , they are playing badminton by the garage."

3 Fill in the verbs (simple present, present progressive).

Mrs Ward is an old woman.

a) Every morning she .... (get up) at eight o'clock.

b) She (make) .... breakfast and .... (drink) some tea.

c) After breakfast she .... (take) her dog Toby for a walk.

d) Look, now she (leave)...................................... her house and she

.... (walk) to the park.

e) It is 8.10 now and a lot of children .... (run) to school. Their

lessons .... (start) at 9 o'clock every day.

f) On Friday school .... (finish) at 3 o'clock.

g) Pupils in England .... (wear) school uniforms. They

.... (eat) lunch at school, too.

h) Now Mrs Ward .... (wait) for Toby. He

.... (run) across the grass.

i) There is a little girl with a ball. She .... (play) with it.

j) At this moment Toby .... (catch) the ball and

Mrs Ward .... (laugh).

k) At 10 o'clock Mrs Ward .... (go) home again and

.... (read) the newspaper.

l) Look. She .... (do) the crossword puzzle.

A birthday party (Katie trifft ihre Freundin Lucy). 4

a)	Sie fragt Lucy, ob sie auch eine	Katie:“ ....
	Einladung zu Rachels Geburts-	....
	tagsparty hat.	..............................?”
b)	Lucy bejaht dies natürlich.	Lucy: “ ....
	Rachel ist ihre Freundin.	....
c)	Katie fragt Lucy, ob sie ein	Katie: ....”
	Geschenk für Rachel hat.	..............................?”
d)	Lucy antwortet, daß sie keines	Lucy: “ ....
	hat. Sie muß eine Schallplatte	....
	oder ein tolles Buch kaufen.	..............................”
e)	Sie fragt Katie, ob sie mitkommt.	“ ....?”
f)	Katie bedauert. Sie muß nach	Katie:“ ....
	Hause gehen. Ihre Mutter ist	....
	krank und wartet auf sie, und	..............................?”
	Katie muß ihr helfen.	....
g)	Lucy schlägt vor, daß sie sich	Lucy: “ ....
	morgen Abend um 7 Uhr treffen.	....
h)	Katie ist einverstanden und	Katie: “ ....”
	verabschiedet sich.	....

Wie sagst Du, wenn 5

a) Patrick ganz verrückt auf Schokolade ist.
b) er nicht alle Kuchen essen soll.
c) er die Schachtel dort holen soll.
d) er um halb 5 aufstehen muß.
e) er Gitarre lernt.

4. Test

1 Dictation.

Katie Potter is a pretty girl of twelve with long black hair and big blue eyes. She has got a lot of boy-friends. At the moment she's on holiday with her parents, her sister and her brother. They are staying at a small hotel in the north of England.

This afternoon she's writing a picture postcard to Patrick Davenport, one of her neighbours at home and her new boy-friend. She's telling him that her holidays are very boring. She is always watching TV or listening to tapes.

There is a small park where she sometimes goes for a walk with her parents. She hasn't got any friends there, so she wants to be back at home.

2 Fill in the pronouns and possessive adjectives.

a) Katie and her sister Emma take .... bikes and ride away.

b) They ride over to.. uncle's house.

c) They can see .... in the garden.

d) They say: " .... uncle is at home. We like to see .... and he is very happy to see ...."

e) Uncle's daughter Susan is in .... room upstairs.

f) Susan can't find .... guitar. Can you see .... ?

g) .... place is in the cupboard.

h) After five minutes Susan finds .... instrument.

Simple present or present progressive tense? 3

a) Look. James Collins, the policeman.............................. (stand) in the street.

He .... (stand) there every morning and evening.

b) In the morning the boys often .... (hurry) to school. It is 9 o'clock

now and they .... (hurry)

c) James often .... (watch) television. At the moment he

.... (watch) a cowboy film.

d) "Jenny, what .... (do) there in the garden?"

– "I .... (repair) my bike."

e) James sometimes .... (play) the guitar.

Listen, he................................. (play) a wonderful song.

f) Lucy always .... (wear) nice dresses.

Now she .... (wear) a red dress.

g) On weekdays Mr Ward.. (go) to work by car.

Mrs Ward.............................. (go) shopping at the moment.

h) Rachel never .... (help) her mother with the housework.

But now she............................. (help) Simon with his bike.

4 Say it in English.

Du erzählst einem Freund auf der Party etwas über dich.

a) Du erzählst ihm, daß du im September Geburtstag hast.

".."

b) Du sagst ihm, daß du deine Freunde oft am Wochenende triffst.

".."

c) Du erwähnst, daß ihr machmal am Samstag zum Schwimmen geht.

".."

d) Du fügst hinzu, daß du am Sonntag gewöhnlich um 10 Uhr ins Bett gehst.

".."

e) Du sagst ihm, daß deine Familie in den Ferien oft nach Frankreich fährt.

".."

f) Du fügst hinzu, daß du eine große Geburtstagsparty im Garten gibst.

".."

g) Du erzählst ihm, daß die Party am Nachmittag in einem Zelt stattfindet.

".."

h) Du sagst ihm, daß ihr eine Menge Getränke und Essen im Supermarkt einkaufen wollt.

".."

5. Test

Dictation. 1

I have got an interesting book. It's about a magician. His name is Bruno. Bruno doesn't live in a house or a flat. He has got a big green, orange and yellow van with a blue bed and other furniture in the back.
Sometimes you can find him in a town centre or in a park among the old trees, sometimes he travels from one place to another. Of course, Bruno does a lot of magic when he is in town. People come to watch him do his fantastic tricks.
For example, he opens a small grey box and when you look into it you cannot see anything. But the next time he opens it there are fourteen white mice, his favourite cat or a guitar in it. It's very funny.

Make sentences with the genitive. 2

a) My .... (friend, name) is Bruno.

b) .... (Bruno, van) is funny.

c) The .... (colour, his bed) is blue.

d) Bruno often rides his .... (friends, bikes).

e) The .... (boy, guitar) is brown.

f) The .... (children, shoes) are red.

g) Bruno likes the .... (women, dresses).

3 Correct these sentences. Give the negative.

a) Bruno is a lorry driver.

No, he ....

b) He sleeps in a big bedroom.

No, ...

c) You can find him on the playing-field.

No, ...

d) He works in the afternoon.

No, ...

e) He always stays in town.

No, ...

4 Translate.

a) Die Potters besuchen Bruno manchmal im Park.

....

b) Bruno wohnt in einem alten Auto.

....

c) Manchmal spielt er Gitarre.

....

d) Er ist nicht faul. Er liegt nicht oft in der Sonne.

....

e) Warum mögen die Kinder Bruno?

....

f) Ich glaube, sie mögen ihn, weil er so lustig ist.

....

Make questions. 5

a) Bruno and his dog are sitting in the park.

. . . .

b) Bruno is playing the guitar at the moment.

. . . .

c) Bruno hasn't got a lot of money in the bank.

. . . .

d) He has got some coins in his purse.

. . . .

e) Bruno can't buy a new guitar because it is so expensive.

. . . .

f) A new guitar costs £100.

. . . .

g) His old guitar is black.

. . . .

h) The children come to see Bruno.

. . . .

i) It's a quarter past four now.

. . . .

j) Two girls are listening to Bruno's songs.

. . . .

k) Bruno's dog is listening too.

. . . .

6. Test

1 Make sentences.

a) often / Katie and Emma / argue

. . . .

b) argue about / the colour / their room / of / now / they

. . . .

c) Emma's records / sometimes / Katie / listen to

. . . .

d) make / at the moment / a fence / their father

. . . .

e) it / look / paint / he

. . . .

2 Fill in the prepositions.

above (over) • for • between
next to (2) • in front of • across • along

a) The Potter's garage is . . . .

their house. The car is . . . . the garage.

b) Emma's room is . . . . the kitchen.

The front door is . . . . the kitchen and the living-room.

c) Emma is standing . . . . the garden wall; she is looking . . . . her ball.

d) Mrs Potter is walking . . . . the street. A bus is coming . . . . the street.

Find the questions. 3

a) Mrs Potter works in an office.

. . . .

b) The children leave home at seven o'clock.

. . . .

c) No, they don't walk to the station.

. . . .

d) Katie and David buy sandwiches because they are hungry.

. . . .

e) David does his homework in the afternoon.

. . . .

f) Yes, he learns French at school.

. . . .

g) Mr and Mrs Potter buy two books.

. . . .

h) Yes, the books are very interesting.

. . . .

i) Mr Potter's car is still in the garage.

. . . .

j) Their car is blue.

. . . .

k) Mr Potter often takes his wife to town in his car.

. . . .

4 Make negative sentences.

a) David sleeps in the garage.

No, ...

b) Mr Potter does all the housework.

No, ...

c) Katie and her sister eat lunch in the bathroom.

No, ...

d) David has got a car.

No, ...

e) Mr Potter and his family live in a flat.

No, ...

5 Wie sagst du, wenn du wissen willst,

a) ob Frau Potters Mann Mechaniker ist.

....

b) was Herr Potter für eine Freizeitbeschäftigung hat.

....

c) wieviel Geld Katie hat.

....

d) ob Katie mit dem Bus oder dem Rad zur Schule fährt.

....

e) ob deine Uhr richtig geht.

....

7. Test

Dictation. 1

Dear Patrick,

Many thanks for your postcard. How are you? We are all fine here.

We don't live in a flat, but we have got our own house. Our house is nice.

My bedroom is next to the bathroom and above the kitchen. Under my parents' bedroom there is the dining-room. The dog likes sleeping in its basket on the floor. It's next to the fireplace. In the evening we all like watching television in the living-room. I must buy new shoes. You can find them in the boys' department of the big store in Market Street. The store has got five floors. On the fifth floor there is the girls' department. Downstairs you can find the men's department. Upstairs on the fourth floor you can buy pets – budgies, hamsters, mice.

My sister Emma has got a goldfish. My sister's room is not very big. Darren and Jenny go to her birthday party. Her friends' present is a white mouse.

Please write soon.

Yours,
David

Explain in a sentence. 2

a) A postcard is something ....

b) A bedroom is ....

c) A dining-room is ....

d) The kitchen is ....

e) A budgie is ....

f) A store is ....

3 Fill in the pronouns / possessive adjectives.

A visit.

a) Here are Mr and Mrs Moore. . . . .

come to visit the Potters because . . . .

are . . . . friends.

b) Mrs Moore has got a bag under . . . .

arm. She is wearing . . . . new dress.

c) Mr Moore is standing behind . . . . is wearing an anorak, but . . . . . is not new.

d) Katie and David are in the garden with . . . . bikes. Can you see

. . . . at the gate.

e) Mrs Moore: "Hallo David, are . . . . parents at home?"

f) David: "Hallo Mrs Moore, how are . . . . ? . . . . am sorry, but . . . . parents

are not in. We can't find . . . . Perhaps. . . . . are doing the shopping.

Mum often buys pizza for . . . . We like. . . . . very much."

g) Mrs Moore : "And what about that car in front of . . . . garage.

Isn't . . . . father's car?"

h) Katie : "Of course not. . . . . is the Clays' car. Come in, and wait for . . . . parents

with . . . . will be back soon."

What are their plans? (Use a form of 'going to'). 4

a) Mrs Moore / wear her new hat / on Sunday

. . . .

b) She and her husband / have a cup of tea

. . . .

c) The children / play football / in the back garden

. . . .

d) Father / come with them / to the final match / on Saturday

. . . .

e) David and Emma / ride their new bikes / at the weekend

. . . .

f) Mr Moore / wash his car / in front of the house

. . . .

g) Sandra and Simon / come to the party / ?

. . . .

h) All their friends / have a good time / at the party

. . . .

i) They all / go home together

. . . .

j) They / not stay / overnight

. . . .

8. Test

1 Dictation.

On Sunday the Potters are giving a dinner-party.

At ten o'clock there are a lot of people in the Potters' hall. The Wards are taking off their coats. Mrs Ward is giving Mrs Potter a nice present in blue paper. Mr Davenport is talking to Mr Clay because he wants to know all about his friend's new expensive car.

But now they are all hungry and they go into the dining-room. Mrs Potter brings the meal on a big tray. First they have rice salad with eggs, toast and butter. Then they eat chops with potatoes. And afterwards they can choose between chocolate cake and ice-cream with strawberries.

After dinner they have a cup of coffee or tea in the living-room. Of course, they don't watch television. Mr Robinson tells them about a terrible film.

When they go home again Mrs Ward says to Mrs Potter "Thank you very much for that wonderful day. Next week you must come and visit us."

2 Find the opposites.

a) Mr Ward's car is not <u>expensive</u>, it is. . . . .

b) The family all <u>go into</u> the dining-room. Mrs Potter . . . . the kitchen.

c) Mrs Potter carries a <u>big</u> tray, David brings a . . . . plate.

d) <u>After</u> dinner they have a cup of coffee, but they have a cup of tea . . . .

they go to bed.

e) The Potters live in a <u>new</u> house. The Parkers live in an . . . . windmill.

f) Emma is <u>closing</u> the door, but she is . . . . the window.

g) The bathroom is <u>upstairs</u>, but the kitchen is . . . .

Make negative sentences. Use 'not'. 3

a) The Potters live in Manchester. They .... in London.

b) They have got a nice little house, but they .... a large garden with trees and flowers.

c) Their son David plays the piano; his sister Emma .... an instrument. Her hobby is knitting.

d) David has tea for breakfast; he .... coffee.

e) He always does his homework in the evening. He .... it in the afternoon.

f) The girls watch TV in the evenings; they .... to the radio.

g) Their parents read the newspaper every day; they .... comics.

Find the questions. 4

a) ....?
Yes, David goes swimming every week.

b) ....?
No, they don't do their homework in the evening.

c) ....?
No, Emma doesn't stay in bed.

d) ....?
Yes, we collect stamps.

e) ....?
Yes, you are a good tennis player.

5 Make correct sentences.

a) work / at the weekends / Mrs Clay / in a department store

. . . .

b) in the garden / the boys / on Sunday / play / football / not

. . . .

c) the car / on Sundays / wash / Mr Potter / ?

. . . .

6 Complete.

a) We . . . . (have) a maths test at school yesterday. It . . . . (be, not) a good start to the week. The questions . . . . (be) difficult.

b) After school Simon . . . . (come) round to our house, and we . . . . (do) our homework together.

c) Last Wednesday I . . . . (play) table tennis. I . . . . (play, not) well, and I . . . . (lose) the game.

d) It . . . . (rain) last Thursday. Mum . . . . (take) me to school in the car.

e) In the evening I . . . . (watch) a film about monsters. I . . . . (like, not) it, but my sister . . . . (enjoy) it very much.

f) Last Saturday I (wash) the car and . . . . (get) a pound from Dad. . . . . (you, wash) your parents' car, too?

Wörterliste
ENGLISCH – DEUTSCH

accident	Unfall
across	(quer) über
again	wieder, nochmal
along	entlang
a lot of	viel(e), eine Menge
already	schon
always	immer
animal	Tier
angry	ärgerlich
apple juice	Apfelsaft
arrive	ankommen
autumn	Herbst
bag	Tasche
because	weil
beautiful	schön
beer	Bier
belong to	gehören
bark	bellen
break	Pause
broken	kaputt
brush	Bürste
budgie	Wellensittich
call	anrufen
carry	tragen, befördern
capital	Hauptstadt
cherry	Kirsche
change	wechseln
choose	wählen
Christmas	Weihnachten
clean	säubern
coast	Küste
climb	klettern
come along	mitkommen
cross	überqueren
cupboard	Schrank
curtain	Vorhang
date	Datum
dirty	schmutzig
do the dishes	Geschirr spülen
doll	Puppe
donkey	Esel
draw	zeichnen
dress	Kleid
drink	Getränk, trinken
empty	leer
enjoy	genießen, gern tun
everything	alles
exercise book	Heft
expensive	teuer
fetch	holen
fill in	einsetzen
fit (into)	(hinein) passen
flat	Wohnung
form teacher	Klassenlehrer
free time	Freizeit
French	französisch
fun	Spaß
funny	spaßig, lustig
glove	Handschuh
glass	Glas
go by bus	mit dem Bus fahren
go shopping	zum Einkaufen gehen
great	großartig
guest	Gast
happen	geschehen
hard (try ~)	tüchtig, hart
have fun	sich vergnügen
hospital	Krankenhaus
hour	Stunde
hurry	sich beeilen
husband	Ehemann

idea	Idee
ill	krank
indoors	im Haus
joke	Witz
jump	springen
just	gerade
knee	Knie
know	wissen, kennen
leave	verlassen, abfahren
lend	leihen
lesson	Unterrichtsstunde
lie	liegen
lift (give a ~)	mitnehmen
listen to	zuhören
lovely	nett
living-room	Wohnzimmer
lunch	Mittagessen
meat	Fleisch
map	Landkarte
middle	Mitte
mistake	Fehler
near	in der Nähe, nahe
neighbour	Nachbar
need	brauchen
noise	Lärm
noisy	laut
office	Büro
orange juice	Orangensaft

pair	Paar
~ of shoes	ein Paar Schuhe
park	parken
peach	Pfirsich
pear	Birne
pencil	Bleistift
pencil case	Federmäppchen
pick	pflücken
picture	Bild
playing field	Spielplatz
pleased	froh
prepare	vorbereiten
pub	Wirtshaus
quiet	ruhig
record	Schallplatte
record-player	Plattenspieler
ride a bike	radfahren
save	sparen
satchel	Schultasche
secretary	Sekretarin
scarf	Schal
sausage	Wurst
seat	Sitz(platz)
shop window	Schaufenster
shop assistant	Verkäufer(in)
shoe	Schuh
shelf; pl. shelves	Regal
slice	Scheibe
shirt	Hemd
skirt	Rock
sometimes	manchmal
spend	ausgeben
slot-machine	Automat
stolen	gestohlen
strawberry	Erdbeere
sweets	Süßigkeiten
stay	bleiben

take off	ausziehen (Kleidung)
teach	unterrichten
three times	dreimal
terrible	furchtbar
thank	danken
throw	werfen
traffic	Verkehr
traffic lights	Verkehsampel
toy	Spielzeug
trousers	Hose
try	versuchen
too	auch
umbrella	Schirm
understand	verstehen
uncle	Onkel
usually	gewöhnlich
vehicle	Fahrzeug
village	Dorf
visit	besuchen, Besuch
walk	spazierengehen, Spaziergang
wait for	warten auf
wall	Mauer
wear	tragen, anziehen
weather	Wetter
what is it like?	wie ist es?
worry	sich sorgen
wrong	falsch
yellow	gelb
youth club	Jugendclub

Wörterliste
DEUTSCH – ENGLISCH

ankommen	arrive
antworten	answer
anrufen	ring, call
aufstehen	get up
aufräumen	tidy up
abschreiben	copy
besuchen	visit
Bier	beer
billig	cheap
Bleistift	pencil
Brieffreund	penfriend
Büro	office
Dialog	dialogue
Dorf	village
dürfen	may, can
eigen, eigenes,	own
eigener	own
einkaufen gehen	go shopping
Einladung	invitation
erklären	explain
Essen	food
fahren (mit dem Bus)	go (by bus)
Fahrrad	bike
Fahrrad fahren	go by bike
fernsehen	watch television (TV)
Ferien	holidays
fischen gehen	go fishing
französisch	French
Geburtstag	birthday
gehören	belong (to)
Geschenk	present
Geschirr spülen	do the dishes
Getränk	drink

gewöhnlich	usually
Glas	glass
glauben	believe
Hauptstadt	capital
Hausaufgaben machen	do homework
Heft	exercise book
Herbst	autumn
hoch	high
holen	fetch
Idee	idea
immer	always
immer noch	still
jeder	every
jung	young
Kalender	calendar
Kasten	box
kämmen	comb
kaufen	buy
Kirsche	cherry
Kleid	dress
Krankenwagen	ambulance
Lastwagen	lorry
läuten	ring
leihen	lend
lesen	read
lustig	funny
manchmal	sometimes
Mechaniker	mechanic
mögen	like
näher	nearer
natürlich	of course
nie	never
Nummer	number
nur	only
Onkel	uncle
Pfirsich	peach
Pudel	poodle
putzen	clean
reinigen	clean
reparieren	repair
Salat	salad
schmutzig	dirty
Schuh	shoe
spanisch	Spanish
Spielplatz	playing-field
Tasche	bag
Taschengeld	pocket money
toll	great
treffen	meet
Urlaub (in ~ fahren)	holiday (go on holiday)
Vereinigtes Königreich	United Kingdom
verlassen	leave
Vetter	cousin
warum	why
warten (auf)	wait (for)
weit	far
wieviel	how much?
wie viele	how many?
Wolkenkratzer	skyscraper
Wörterheft	vocabulary book
Zelt	tent
Zucker	sugar

Wörterliste
DEUTSCH – ENGLISCH

Lernbereich
GRAMMATIK (S. 8-50)

1.
a) an, a **b)** an, a **c)** a, an **d)** a, an **e)** a, an **f)** a, an **g)** a, an **h)** an, a **i)** an, a **j)** A, An **k)** a, an **l)** an, an.

TIP: *an hour – das 'h' ist stumm.*

2.
a) girls, boys, babies, ladies **b)** cherries, apples, peaches, shelves **c)** dresses, skirts, coats, shoes **d)** potatoes, eggs, oranges, strawberries **e)** toys, dolls, balls, planes **f)** buses, vans, lorries, taxis.

TIP: *boy***s***, toy***s** *– vor dem y ist ein Vokal*
*shel***ves** *– besondere Schreibung → 2. Lernjahr*

3.
a) children **b)** women **c)** men **d)** policemen **e)** teeth **f)** feet

4.
a) I have three apples, five peaches and lots of cherries. **b)** In front of the supermarket there are two cars, three buses and four lorries. **c)** The children need new clothes. **d)** My mother must buy potatoes, apples, oranges and tomatoes.

5.
a) This, that **b)** These, those **c)** Those, this **d)** These, that **e)** This, those **f)** These, Those.

TIP: *that apple = der Apfel (dort), jener Apfel*

6.
a) This book is red. What colour is that book? **b)** These are my pencils. Those pencils belong to Paul. **c)** This is an old house. Those houses in the street are new.
d) Are those your friends? Yes. They're my friends from London. **e)** What's this? It's my photograph album.

TIP: **They're** *– weil 'friends' Plural ist*

7.
a) The boy's shirt is new. **b)** Jane's scarf is green. **c)** The man's shoes are black.
d) The Browns' neighbours are friendly. **e)** The girls' hats are yellow. **f)** The children's T-shirts are funny. **g)** The lady's dress is pretty. **h)** The boys' trousers are blue. **i)** Our friends' house is in the country. **j)** The women's umbrellas are red.

8.
a) The church of our village is very old. The roof of the church is red. **b)** The coast of England is beautiful. The parks of London are very nice. **c)** The rooms of our school are big. The windows of this room are small. **d)** The seats of Peter's car are blue.

The doors of his car are black. **e)** The station of our town is new. The locomotive of the train is red.

9.

a) cigarettes **b)** bread **c)** jeans **d)** tea **e)** potatoes **f)** cake **g)** sweets **h)** milk **i)** lemonade **j)** toys.

10.

a) The school of our village is very small. There is the church of our village. **b)** These are the girls' books. Where is your brother's bike? **c)** Is football your friend's hobby? My best friend's name is Robert. **d)** Dover is in the south of England. The capital of Scotland is Edinburgh. **e)** This is not Mr Brown's car. The streets of our village are very narrow. **f)** Can you bring me a glass of milk? Give me a pound of potatoes, please. **g)** My aunt's house is at the end of the road. The number of the house is 20. **h)** This is not my parents' house. My parents' house is at the park.

11.

a) children **b)** girls **c)** The Millers' shop **d)** These are **e)** men's hats **f)** My parents' house.

12.

a) me **b)** your **c)** He, his **d)** her, her **e)** It, it (z.B. ein Tier) **f)** We, our, us **g)** You, your, you **h)** their, them.

TIP: you – heißt, je nach Sinnzusammenhang, du / ihr; dich bzw. dir / euch.

13.

a) her **b)** your **c)** my, my, his **d)** your, my, His **e)** her, Her **f)** Her **g)** her **h)** their **i)** his **j)** my, your **k)** My, my.

14.

a) you **b)** I, me **c)** your **d)** it, My **e)** them, They **f)** them **g)** them, I, He, his, him **h)** I, him, He, he, us **i)** my / our, He, us, his **j)** you, his, She, us, her.

15.

a) My bike is new. **b)** Can I have your bike? **c)** Mary has her books under the table. **d)** She must write her name on her exercise books. **e)** Do your parents live in their own house? **f)** I've got a new T-shirt, it's red.

16.

a) Tom often washes his new car. His sister helps him. **b)** They wash their car every week. Its colour is blue. **c)** This is our car. It is a Rover. **d)** Susan and Jill are my sisters. Can you see them? **e)** They are in their room. Their room isn't very big. **f)** Susan gives Jill her English textbook and her vocabulary book. Then they do their homework.

*TIP: They **do** their homework – Sie machen ihre Hausaufgabe.*

17.
a) aren't, are, is **b)** Is, is, is, are, aren't **c)** Are, aren't, are **d)** Are, am not, am.

18.
a) What's the time? (What time is it?) – It is 2 o'clock. **b)** Are you tired? – No, I'm not tired. **c)** Where are Bill and Mike? – They are at school. **d)** Is Susan at school too? – No, she is at home. **e)** How old are the girls? – Susan is 12, Anne is 11 **f)** How are the girls? – Susan is fine, Ann is ill.

19.
a) has, have, **b)** have, has **c)** have, have **d)** has, hasn't (got) **e)** have, has **f)** has, have.

20.
a) Have you (got) a penfriend? – Yes, I've (got) a penfriend in America. **b)** Have you (got) a bike, Mike? – Yes, I've (got) a new black bike. **c)** Has your friend (got) a room of her own, Susan? No, she hasn't (got) her own room. – Jill and her sister have (got) a room together. **d)** Our school has (got) 500 pupils. – How many pupils has your school (got)**?**

21.
a) am going, going **b)** are writing, You're writing **c)** is running, He's running; is sitting, He's sitting **d)** is reading, She's reading; is eating, She's eating **e)** is jumping. it's jumping **f)** are coming, We're coming **g)** are waiting, You're waiting **h)** are playing, They're playing; are swimming, They're swimming.

TIP: *write/ writing, come/ coming – Das stumme 'e' am Wortende fallt weg run/ running, sit/ sitting, swim/ swimming – Der Schlußkonsonant wird verdoppelt.*

22.
a) is doing, is not listening **b)** Is Peter listening, is writing **c)** is Judy not doing, is helping **d)** is coming, is going **e)** are … hurrying, are running **f)** are making, are playing.

23.
a) I am washing up. **b)** Tom is watching TV. **c)** Susan is writing a letter. **d)** Peter is tidying his room. **e)** Father is repairing the car. **f)** My friend is doing his homework. **g)** What are you doing?**h)** What are you reading? **i)** Where are you going? **j)** Why are you working? **k)** Who are you ringing (phoning)? **l)** What are you eating?

24.
a) wake up, don't get up **b)** speak, don't know **c)** reads, doesn't read **d)** makes, doesn't drink **e)** rains, doesn't rain **f)** go, don't stay **g)** watch, don't go **h)** play, don't win.

25.
a) do, do, go, clean **b)** Does father make, makes, prepares **c)** does school … start, begins **d)** do the children do, play **e)** watches, does, comes **f)** do the children do, read, listen.

26.

a) I get up at six every day. **b)** I leave home at half past seven. **c)** I always take the bus. **d)** I arrive at school at 8 o'clock. **e)** I don't always do my homework. **f)** My friend often helps me. **g)** After school we sometimes play basketball. **h)** I like basketball.
i) Some of my friends don't like it. **j)** We often go to the cinema in the evening (In the evening we often go to the cinema). **k)** My big brother drives us home in his car.
i) We go to Scotland every year. There we visit my aunt Jane.

27.

a) Patrick always gets up at 7 o'clock. He tidies his room every day. He often walks to school. He sometimes goes by bike. **b)** Rachel works at a supermarket. She doesn't work on Sunday. Rachel speaks English and understands a little French. She doesn't speak German. **c)** Darren has (got) three sisters and a brother. His brother has (got) lots of friends. Darren's parents live in a big house. Darren's mother doesn't work. **d)** Steven does his homework in the afternoon. Then he meets his friends. They often go to town. Steven doesn't play football. **e)** Does James often read books? – No, he doesn't. He doesn't like books. Why does he often watch TV? He likes interesting films. **f)** Does Jenny play an instrument? She plays the guitar, but she doesn't often play. Why doesn't she often play? She helps her mother in the kitchen. **g)** Tony washes himself every morning. He cleans his teeth and combs his hair. In the afternoon he goes to the playing field. But he doesn't play football.

28.

a) is swimming, swims **b)** is playing, plays **c)** is going, goes **d)** are listening, don't listen **e)** are playing, don't often play **f)** is watching, watches **g)** is going, goes.

29.

am just sitting, is shining, am writing, want, don't write, am not, am having, have, is playing, hear, play, don't like, am enjoying, is, tells, is calling, calls, wants, hope.

TIP: *I'm having tea – ich trinke (gerade) Tee*

30.

a) What are you doing? – I'm reading a book. **b)** Where are you going? – I'm going to the supermarket. **c)** What are you doing? – We're writing a letter. **d)** When does the train arrive? – It usually arrives at half past eight. **e)** I go to school by bike every day, because it isn't very far. **f)** I often play tennis, but I don't play with my sister.

31.

a) Where are you going, Mary? **b)** I'm going to the cafe. **c)** Do you often go out? **d)** I always meet my friends on Wednesday. **e)** Look. Here comes Jenny. She's going shopping. **f)** I usually shop in town on Saturday. **g)** I sometimes help my mother. My father never goes shopping. He usually gets up at ten o'clock on Saturday. **h)** Is your sister at home? **i)** No, she's riding her bike. She always takes her bike to get to school. **j)** What is your brother doing? **k)** He is sitting in his room and doing his homework. **l)** Does he always do his homework in his room? **m)** Yes, he does.

32.
a) writes **b)** is running **c)** listens **d)** go **e)** don't play (aren't playing) **f)** I watch.

33.
a) are going to have, are going to invite **b)** is going to bring, are not only going to listen, are going to dance **c)** is going to prepare, is going to buy **d)** are going to have, is going to eat **e)** is going to buy, is not going to buy **f)** are you going to do, Are you going to have.

34.
a) stopped **b)** landed **c)** repaired **d)** watched **e)** fetched **f)** didn't enjoy **g)** stayed **h)** did it rain **h)** did Kevin repair **i)** didn't help.

35.
a) was **b)** had **c)** did **d)** went **e)** read **f)** spoke **g)** saw **h)** took **i)** left **j)** were **k)** got up **l)** ate.

36.
a) Can you help me? **b)** Can / May I have your pencil? **c)** Can I repair your bike? **d)** Must you help at home? **e)** May / Can you come this afternoon? **f)** I can't come. **g)** I must help my mother. h) You can play with my brother. **i)** You can come at four o'clock. **j)** My brother can't play volleyball.

37.
a) Can / May I go out? **b)** Can you explain that in German? **c)** Can / May I take your bike, Dad? **d)** I can't answer it. **e)** May / Can I help you? **f)** I can't come.

38.
a) Tony can ... **b)** Sheila can't ride ... **c)** She can ride ... **d)** May we watch ... ?

39.
a) Is **b)** Are **c)** Have you got **d)** Are you reading **e)** Can **f)** Must **g)** Are **h)** Were.

40.
a) Does Tom eat an apple? **b)** Does Geoff like music? **c)** Do the girls get up early? **d)** Does Mr Brown drive to his office? **e)** Do Mary and Jenny listen to pop records? **f)** Did father do all the housework yesterday?

41.
a) Is your brother at home? Can you play tennis? Have you got a new bike? Are your parents in town? **b)** Do you go to school by bike? Do you play rugby? Must you learn a lot? Can you speak French?

42.
a) Does the boy eat **b)** Can Peter swim? **c)** Have Susan and her friend **d)** Must you help **e)** Does Anne speak **f)** Do you come to town?

43.

a) Where does Geoff sit? **b)** When does Bill get up? **c)** How do the Browns get to work? **d)** Who (Whom) does Mary often meet? **e)** What does Mr Brown drink? **f)** Why can't Bill go to school? **g)** What does Susan write? **h)** When must they be at the bus stop?

44.

a) Where do the Browns live? **b)** What have they got there? **c)** What does Mrs Brown like? **d)** When does Jane go to the judo club? **e)** Who (Whom) does she meet there? **f)** What does Jane like? **g)** Why does she often go out on Saturday? **h)** What does Jane take? **i)** Who (Whom) did Mr Brown visit in New York last summer? **j)** How long did he stay in America?

45.

a) When do you go to school? Where do you live? Do you go by bus? **b)** How old are you? What do you do in your holidays? Why do you work at a shop? **c)** What are you doing, Jane? Which book are you reading? What's your brother doing? **d)** When did you go to London, Jim? What did you do last Sunday? Why didn't you come to the party?

46.

a) Who goes to school at eight? **b)** Whose cousin plays cricket? **c)** How many of Jane's friends live in Manchester? **d)** What stands in front of the house? **e)** Who gets up at seven? **f)** Who got up at half past six? **g)** What happened?

47.

a) Aren't you from Scotland? **b)** Haven't you got a pen-friend in Italy? **c)** Don't you read a book from time to time? **d)** What don't you understand? **e)** Why doesn't she sleep? **f)** Where can't they park their car? **g)** Whose sister doesn't go to the party? **h)** What doesn't fit into this bag?

TIP: – Achte besonders auf die verneinten Subjektfragen g) und h)

48.

a) What are you playing? Where are the girls going? Who's running over there? What's Paul doing? **b)** When does the train leave? Where do the Potters live? Why does Jack play cricket? How many balls does Martin buy? **c)** How old is Susan? Where can we play tennis? When must Peter help his father? How much is this record? **d)** Who plays with Barbara? Whose sister lives in town? How many girls go to the party? What stops in front of the school? **e)** Who doesn't speak English? Who doesn't come to the birthday party? How many children don't go to school? Why doesn't Peter help us?

49.
a) When does Betty come? **b)** Where does Patrick live? **c)** Where did you go? **d)** How do you come? **e)** How many boys play? **f)** Who gets up?

50.
a) Geoff plays the guitar. **b)** Jane draws a picture. **c)** Mr Brown reads the newspaper. **d)** The girls bake a cake. **e)** Tom plays in the garden. **f)** We must write a dictation.

51.
a) Tom never eats cornflakes. **b)** Jack always goes to bed before ten. **c)** The girls usually go to school by bus. **d)** Susan must often help her mother. **e)** James is often ill. **f)** We can always park our car here. **g)** The boys often played football.

52.
a) Peter plays football every day. **b)** Susan never goes shopping on Sunday. **c)** Mr Brown drives to work at seven o'clock. **d)** They often visit their parents in Scotland. **e)** The children usually go to bed at ten o'clock. **f)** Susan plays the piano every Friday.

53.
a) Patrick washes the car in the garage on Fridays. **b)** Stuart watches television in the living-room in the evenings. **c)** Dawn plays pop music in her room in the evening.
d) James plays football in the garden on Saturdays. **e)** The Potters have lots of flowers in their garden in summer. **f)** Darren often goes to Wales on holiday. **g)** Katie goes to the swimming-pool every Saturday. **h)** Mr Robinson goes shopping at the supermarket on Monday.

TIP: Du könntest auch mit dem Adverb der Zeit beginnen, z.B. ***On Fridays*** *Patrick washes the car in the garage.*

54.
a) I always go to school by bus. On Saturday I never go to school. On Sunday I often go to the cinema. I sometimes go swimming in the afternoon. **b)** Tom often watches TV in the evening. On Saturday he always plays football. Tom is always friendly. He sometimes reads a book in his holidays. **c)** In summer Mr Brown always works in the garden. On Sunday he sometimes goes fishing. The Browns never go to the cinema. They often sit in their living-room. **d)** Petra often goes for a walk in the afternoon. She sometimes meets Susan in the park. The weather is often cold in summer. Petra always wears a coat in winter. **e)** I saw a film on TV yesterday. I often watched TV last week. On Monday I went to the supermarket with a friend. We bought a new CD there.

TIP: Es gibt auch andere richtige Lösungen. z.B. I never go to school on Saturday.

55.
a) My sister often draws **b)** Our English teacher is never **c)** I always read **d)** We play in our club every Tuesday (Every Tuesday we play in our club). **e)** They sometimes go **f)** In the evenings he takes (He takes his dog for a walk in the evenings).

S. 45-50

Lernbereich GRAMMATIK

Lernbereich
RECHTSCHREIBUNG (S. 53-74)

1.

a) Sweden b) Ireland c) United Kingdom d) Germany e) France f) Switzerland g) Austria h) Italy

i) Ireland, English j) France, French k) Germany, German l) Austria, German

2.

English, London, capital, Great Britain, father, bus driver, mother, housewife,comprehensive school, English, French, German, Monday, Friday, school, Saturday, Sunday, June, summer holidays, August, pen, Paris, France, Christmas holidays, friends, Scotland, autumn.

3.

a) five b) fourteen c) fifteen d) forty e) twenty-two f) thirty-four g) fifty-five h) sixty-eight i)first j)second k) fourth l) fifth m) twenty-first n) thirty-second o) forty-third p) fifty-fourth.

4.

a) good-looking b) dining-room *(auch: dining room)* c) pen-friend *(auch: penfriend)* d) pocket-money *(auch: pocket money)* e) record-player *(auch: record player)* f) swimming-pool *(auch: swimming pool).* g) grandfather h) birthday i) postcard j) homework k) toyshop .l) bathroom m) shop assistant n) police station o) television set p) pet shop q) orange juice r) free time.

TiP: Einige Wörter haben zwei Schreibweisen.

5.

a) I'm, I'm not / you're, you're not, you aren't/ he's, he's not, he isn't / she's, she's not, she isn't / it's, it's not, it isn't / we're, we're not, we aren't / they're, they're not, they aren't b) I've got, I've not got, I haven't got / you've got, you've not got, you haven't got / he's got, he's not got, he hasn't got / we've got,we've not got, we haven't got / they've got, they've not got, they haven't got c) Here's / There's / That's d) What's this? / Where's Bob? / Who's this / Who's got it? e) I can't / I mustn't.

TIP: Du mußt beim Diktat genau zuhören, welche Kurzform du schreiben sollst, z.B. I've not got oder I haven't got.

6.

a) cousin's b) brother's c) boy's d) girls' e) Sandra's f) Mr Miller's g) child's h) man's i) woman's j) children's k) lady's l) parents'

7.

a) pocket money b) Great Britain c) dining-room (auch: dining room) d) children's department e) youth club f) information desk g) grandfather h) French i) police station j) autumn k) skyscraper l)pen-friend (auch: penfriend).

S. 53-59

Lernbereich RECHTSCHREIBUNG

8.
a) French, month **b)** friend, capital **c)** Johnsons', ten years **d)** haven't, it's.

9.
a) boxes **b)** glasses **c)** bushes **d)** dresses **e)** bikes **f)** buses **g)** classes **h)** pencils **i)** potatoes **j)** tomatoes **k)** gets up **l)** watches **m)** goes **n)** washes **o)** fetches **p)** buys **q)** brushes **r)** makes **s)** does **t)** crosses.

10.
a) Tom's books **b)** girl's hat **c)** dresses, women's dresses **d)** girls' hats **e)** man's hat **f)** glasses, Jane's glasses **g)** boxes, boys' boxes **h)** Geoff's, Geoff's friends **i)** Smiths, Smiths' **j)** Who's, It's **k)** He's, Jane's **l)** He's, cassettes.

11.
a) families **b)** days **c)** toys **d)** pennies **e)** hobbies **f)** ponies **g)** cherries **h)** keys **i)** tries **j)** buys **k)** plays **l)** dries up **m)** carries **n)** worries **o)** hurries **p)** cries.

12.
a) coming **b)** dancing **c)** using **d)** choosing **e)** making **f)** living **g)** giving **h)** changing **i)** preparing **j)** arriving.

13.
a) getting **b)** stopping **c)** cutting **d)** running **e)** waiting **f)** hitting **g)** sitting **h)** bringing **i)** putting **j)** preparing.

T I P : Keine Verdoppelung bei wait (Doppelvokal), bring (Konsonant) und prepare (am Ende ist ein -e).

14.
a) Peter buys two pencils and three exercise-books. He often does his homework in the afternoon. **b)** Jane gets up at seven o'clock. She washes herself and combs her hair. She goes to school by bike (on her bike). **c)** Mrs White buys apples, pears, tomatoes and potatoes. She gets (fetches) everything from the supermarket. **d)** Paul has lots of hobbies. He often plays with his toys. He's got two little lorries. **e)** Mother hurries to the supermarket. She carries a big bag. She often buys cherries and oranges. **f)** What's Susan doing? She's dancing with Paul. They're coming nearer. **g)** Mrs Potter is laying the table. The Potters are having lunch. Martin is taking a slice of bread. **h)** Look. Tony is running to the house. Susan is sitting in front of the door. She's waiting for her sister. **i)** Tony repaired his bike yesterday. A car stopped in front of the garage. Susan waited at the door.

15.
Getting / sleeps / coming / stopping.

16.
b) sun **c)** pear **d)** hour **e)** meat **f)** two **g)** write **h)** sea **i)** hear **j)** know

17.
a) two, to, too **b)** his, He's, his **c)** It's, It's, its **d)** There, They're, Their **e)** hear, here, her **f)** know, no, now.

18.
a) who **b)** whose **c)** wrong **d)** hour **e)** knee **f)** write **g)** walk **h)** cupboard **i)** half **j)** daughter **k)** often **l)** right **m)** talk **n)** when **o)** climb **p)** comb **q)** autumn **r)** high.

19.
a) talk, walk **b)** wrong, write **c)** climb, come d) half, calf **e)** hour, house f) who **g)** knife, knee, know **h)** often, listen, late

20.
a) pair **b)** There **c)** sun **d)** It's **e)** meet **f)** Autumn.

21.
a) adjective **b)** knee **c)** sugar **d)** salad **e)** marmalade **f)** Sunday **g)** idea – **England** **h)** shoe **i)** December **j)** model **k)** doctor **l)** telephone **m)** cap **n)** uncle **o)** poodle- **Scotland**

22.
a) music **b)** guitar **c)** object **d)** toilet **e)** wash **f)** calendar **g)** record – **Ireland** h) swim i) lemonade **j)** ambulance **k)** beer **l)** glass – **Wales.**

23.
a) Peter's birthday is in July, Betty's in October. **b)** There are lemonade, beer and coffee at the party. **c)** The Spanish apples are very good. **d)** England, Scotland, Wales and Northern Ireland are the United Kingdom. **e)** Mr White speaks English. He lives in America. **f)** His brother is a doctor in Canada. **g)** The television programme isn't very good. **h)** The grass in our garden is high. **i)** Can you copy the dialogue in a minute? **j)** The telephone is ringing. – It's uncle Paul. **k)** My uncle has got a poodle and a cat. **l)** Patrick likes music; he often plays the guitar.

24.
a) marmalade **b)** telephone **c)** lemonade **d)** secretary **e)** possessive **f)** electric.

25.
It's, getting, too, fourteen, friends, see, becoming, sandwiches, replies, cream, goes, write.

Lernbereich
WORTSCHATZ (S. 78-98)

1.
a) ear **b)** eye **c)** mouth **d)** hair **e)** arm **f)** neck **g)** hand **h)** finger **i)** leg **j)** foot **k)** hat **l)** shirt **m)** trousers **n)** a pair of trousers **o)** a pair of jeans **p)** blouse **q)** coat **r)** dress **s)** skirt **t)** tights **u)** shoes **v)** socks

2.
a) bus **b)** plane **c)** lorry **d)** van **e)** motorbike **f)** bike **g)** caravan **h)** car **i)** chair **j)** armchair **k)** table **l)** desk **m)** cupboard **n)** shelf **o)** bed **p)** clock (watch = Armbanduhr!) **q)** television set **r)** radio **s)** picture **t)** fire-place.

3.
a) bird, budgie, cat, dog, horse, mouse **b)** bread, cake, cheese, egg, marmalade, salad **c)** beer, coffee, lemonade, milk, orange juice, tea

4.
a) hear **b)** listening **c)** hear **d)** see, see **e)** Look **f)** looking **g)** asks **h)** answer **i)** say(s), Tell **j)** answer, speak

5.
a) do **b)** doing, making **c)** do, make **d)** makes **e)** doing, making **f)** wearing, wears **g)** carrying **h)** wears **i)** carry **j)** wears.

6.
a) the board **b)** a tree **c)** homework **d)** the door **e)** flowers **f)** a game **g)** a newspaper **h)** a bike **i)** a photo **j)** the dishes **k)** TV **l)** trousers.

7.
a9) b6) c10) d3) e4) f1) g2 h7) i5) j8).

8.
a) bedroom **b)** bathroom **c)** living-room **d)** dining-room **e)** playing-field **f)** bus stop **g)** satchel **h)** kitchen **i)** cinema **j)** instrument.

9.
a) black – white **b)** clean – dirty **c)** early – late **d)** full – empty **e)** good – bad **f)** left – **right** g) long – short **h)** noisy – quiet **i)** **right** – wrong **j)** old – new **k)** slow – quick **l)** small – big.

TIP: Wichtig ist der Sinnzusammenhang, in dem das Wort benutzt wird, z.B. f) left = links – right = rechts, i) right = richtig – wrong = falsch.

10.
a) sister **b)** girl **c)** daughter **d)** wife **e)** woman **f)** mother **g)** aunt **h)** grandfather.

11.
a) in front of **b)** out of **c)** past **d)** downstairs **e)** without **f)** to **g)** outside **h)** under.

12.
a) sitting **b)** Sit down **c)** shutting **d)** end **e)** get up **f)** put on **g)** saves **h)** buy **i)** hates **j)** coming out **k)** answer **l)** leaves.

13.
a) Who **b)** Where **c)** Why **d)** because **e)** Why **f)** where **g)** Who **h)** Why, because **i)** who **j)** where.

14.
a) still **b)** too **c)** much **d)** always **e)** again **f)** of course **g)** many **h)** altogether **i)** sometimes **j)** Every **k)** but **l)** only.

15.
a) Who can speak English? **b)** Where is the playing-field? **c)** Why does Susan go home? **d)** How much is the book? **e)** How many friends has Tom (got)? **f)** I always get up early. **g)** I sometimes go swimming. **h)** I read every day. **i)** I've got only two books. **j)** My parents are still in London.

16.
a) in; **b)** in; **c)** at; **d)** at; **e)** in; **f)** on

17.
a) Mrs Potter always goes shopping on Saturday. She gets up at 7 o'clock. **b)** Judy's birthday is in May. She gives a big birthday party on 12th May. **c)** Patrick plays ice-hockey in winter and football in summer. The matches are often on Saturday. **d)** In the morning Susan and her brother go to school. In the afternoon they do their homework. **e)** Tom's birthday is on a Sunday. His friends meet on Saturday at 8 o'clock.

18.
a) five past ten **b)** a quarter past eleven **c)** half past seven **d)** a quarter to two **e)** five to eight **f)** three minutes to eight.

19.
a) Judy gets up at half past six. She goes to the bus stop at (a) quarter to eight. **b)** The bus leaves at three minutes to eight. The first lesson begins at twenty past eight.
c) School ends at half past two. Judy is at home at ten to three. **d)** The film begins at (a) quarter past eight. Judy meets her friends in front of the cinema at five to eight.

20.
a) at, in **b)** in, at **c)** on, at **d)** at, on **e)** In, on, on **f)** at, on.

21.
a) The tea is in the cup. **b)** The cup is on the saucer. **c)** The cup is on the table.
d) Martin is not at home. **e)** He is at school. **f)** The toys are in the cupboard. **g)** The book is lying on the floor.

22.
a) into **b)** out of **c)** to **d)** out of, to **e)** out of **f)** across, into.

23.
a) Simon often goes to the cinema. **b)** On Saturday Rachel goes to the disco. **c)** Look. Tom is running across the road. **d)** Peter always goes to school by bike. **e)** Look. Susan is going out of the room. **f)** Peter is throwing the ball across the river. **g)** Mary is translating the text into French. **h)** I am drinking tea out of a red cup. **i)** We often go to England. **j)** The girls are going into their room.

24.
a) of, in, at, by, by **b)** into, On, on, of **c)** of, out of, to, at **d)** on, to, at, in, at **e)** at, at, into, out of **f)** At, at, in, at, in **g)** in, in, at.

25.
a4 b7 c1 d8 e3 f2 g9 h10 i5 j6

26.
a) There is **b)** there are **c)** are there **d)** There are **e)** there is **f)** There are.

27.
a) Billy **b)** twelve **c)** Scotland **d)** Monday **e)** 1 st April **f)** half past ten **g)** It's fine **h)** cornflakes **i)** 5) **j)** brown **k)** twelve **l)** I've got a flu.

28.
a) Where do you come from? Are you English or American? How old are you? What are your hobbies? Have you got any brothers or sisters? **b)** What's the time? What time is it? How are you? How are your parents? Who's your new teacher? When do you get up in the morning? **c)** Have you got a bike? Have you got a garden at home? Have your parents got one or two cars? Have you got a pen-friend? Do you often go to parties?

29.
a) Good morning, Simon. How are you? **b)** Good afternoon, Mr Moore. I'm sorry, but my parents are not at home. **c)** Hallo, Alan. Are you coming to the cinema with me? – I'm sorry, I have got no time. I must help my mother. **d)** Can you come to my birthday party, Emma? – Yes, of course.

Lernbereich
PRÜFUNGSTRAINING (S. 101-124)

1. Test
1. TIPS: Apostroph → Seite 61
Zahlen → Seite 55

2. a) twenty-five minus fifteen is ten **b)** five plus nine is fourteen **c)** thirteen plus four is seventeen **d)** fifty-five minus nineteen is thirty-six **e)** forty-two plus fifty-six is ninety-eight **f)** fifty-five minus fifteen is forty.
3. a) those **b)** this **c)** that, That **d)** those, pairs **e)** pairs, that **f)** pair, these, those, pair.
4. a) tea, coffee, lemonade, cola **b)** bus, train, lorry, van **c)** blue, red, green, black.
5. a) The men are waiting for the buses. **b)** The cars are in the garages. **c)** The women are riding bikes. **d)** The children have oranges. **e)** The boys are eating cakes. **f)** The lorries are in the streets.

2. Test
1. TIPS: Apostroph 's oder Plural -s → Seite 61
-ing Form → Seite 21, 63, 64

2. a) three hundred and sixty-five, fifty-two **b)** third, June, fifth **c)** seasons, spring, autumn, winter **d)** z.B. 1st May, 2nd January, 3rd June, 11th December.
3. a) their **b)** Its, his **c)** her, her **d)** my, your, your **e)** his, their **f)** Our, their.
4. talk to **b)** watch **c)** repair **d)** do **e)** play.
5. a) Hallo, Mr Davenport. May I look at the pets in your shop? **b)** Of course. Have you got a pet? **c)** No, I haven't. My parents have only got a small flat, and we haven't got a garden. **d)** Can I help you in the afternoon? **e)** I'm Katie Potter. I'm twelve and a pupil at Park School. **f)** You must feed and clean the pets. Can you come every Thursday afternoon at three o'clock? **g)** Yes, but I must ask my mother.

3. Test
1. TIPS: -s oder -es → Seite 61
Unterschied zum Deutschen (Sunday, programme, record) → Seite 72

2. a) you **c)** you **d)** me **e)** it **f)** them **g)** us, them.
3. a) gets up **b)** makes, drinks **c)** takes **d)** is leaving, is walking **e)** are running, start **f)** finishes **g)** wear, eat **h)** is waiting, is running **i)** is playing **j)** is catching, is laughing **k)** goes, reads **l)** is doing
4. a) Have you got an invitation to Rachel's birthday party, too? **b)** Yes, of course. Rachel is my friend. **c)** Have you got a present for Rachel? **d)** No, I haven't. I must buy a record or a good book. **e)** Are you coming? **f)** No, sorry. I must go home. My mother is ill, and she is waiting for me. I must help her. **g)** Let's meet (Shall we meet) at seven o'clock tomorrow evening. **h)** Yes, all right. Good-bye.
5. a) Patrick loves chocolate (is crazy about chocolate). **b)** Don't eat all cakes. **c)** Fetch that box, please. **d)** He must get up at half past four. **e)** He is learning the guitar.

4. Test

1. TIPS: Apostroph 's oder Plural -s → Seite 61
-ing Formen → Seite 63-65

2. a) their **b)** their **c)** him **d)** Our, him, us **e)** her **f)** her, it **g)** Its **h)** her.
3. a) is standing, stands **b)** hurry, hurrying **c)** watches, is watching **d)** are you doing, am repairing **e)** plays, is playing **f)** wears, is wearing **g)** goes, is going **h)** helps, is helping.
4. a) My birthday is in September. **b)** I often meet my friends at the weekend. **c)** We sometimes go swimming on Saturday. **d)** On Sundays I usually go to bed at ten o'clock. **e)** My family often goes to France on holiday. **f)** I'm giving a big birthday party in the garden. **g)** The party is in a tent in the afternoon. **h)** We want to buy a lot of drinks and food at the supermarket.

5. Test

1. TIPS: -s oder -es → Seite 60

2. a) friend's name **b)** Bruno's van **c)** colour of his bed **d)** friends' bikes **e)** boy's guitar **f)** children's shoes **g)** women's dresses.
3. a) (he) isn't a lorry driver. **b)** he doesn't sleep in a big bedroom. **c)** you can't find him on the playing-field. **d)** he doesn't work in the afternoon. **e)** he doesn't always stay in town.
4. a) The Potters sometimes visit Bruno in the park. **b)** Bruno lives in an old car. **c)** Sometimes he plays the guitar. **d)** He is not lazy. He doesn't often lie in the sun. **e)** Why do the children like Bruno? **f)** I think, they like him because he is so funny.
5. a) Where are Bruno and his dog sitting? **b)** What is Bruno doing at the moment? **c)** What hasn't Bruno got in the bank? **d)** Where has he got some coins? **e)** Why can't Bruno buy a new guitar? **f)** How much is a new guitar (How much does a new guitar cost)? **g)** What colour is his old guitar? **h)** Who do the children come to see? **i)** What's the time (What time is it)? **j)** Who is listening to Bruno's songs? **k)** Whose dog is listening, too?

6. Test

1. a) Katie and Emma often argue. **b)** They are arguing about the colour of their room now. **c)** Katie sometimes listens to Emma's records. **d)** Their father is making a fence at the moment. **e)** Look, he's painting it.
2. a) next to, in front of **b)** above (over), between **c)** next to, for **d)** across, along.
3.a) Where does Mrs Potter work? **b)** When do the children leave home? **c)** Do they walk to the station? **d)** Why do Katie and David buy sandwiches? **e)** What does David do in the afternoon? f) Does he learn French at school? **g)** How many books do Mr and Mrs Potter buy? **h)** Are the books interesting? **i)** Where is Mr Potter's car? **j)** What colour is their car? **k)** Who does Mr Potter often take to town in his car?
4.a) he doesn't sleep in the garage. **b)** he doesn't do all the housework. **c)** they don't eat lunch in the bathroom. **d)** he hasn't got a car. **e)** they don't live in a flat.
5.a) Is Mrs Potter's husband a mechanic? **b)** What is Mr Potter's favourite pastime? **c)** How much money has Katie (got)? **d)** Does Katie go to school by bus or by bike? **e)** Is my watch right?

7. Test

1.TIPS: Plural -s oder 's genitiv → Seite 61
Präpositionen → Seite 91-95

2.a) you write to your friend. **b)** is the room where you (can) sleep. **c)** the room where you eat. **d)** is the room where you cook **e)** is a bird that can sing. **f)** is a big shop.
3.a) They, they, their **b)** her, her **c)** her, He, it **d)** their, them **e)** your **f)** you, I, my, them, they, us, it **g)** your, it, your **h)** It, our, us, They.
4. a) Mrs Moore is going to wear her new hat on Sunday. **b)** She and her husband are going to have a cup of tea. **c)** The children are going to play football in the back garden. **d)** Father is going to come with them to the final match on Saturday.
e) David and Emma are going to ride their new bikes at the weekend. **f)** Mr Moore is going to wash his car in front of the house. **g)** Are Sandra and Simon going to come to the party? **h)** All their friends are going to have a good time at the party. **i)** They all are going to go home together. **j)** They are not going to stay over night.

8. Test

1. TIPS: Plural -s oder Genitiv -s → Seite 61
Unterschiede zum Deutschen (salad, chocolate, cake, cream) → Seite 71-73

2. a) cheap **b)** comes out of **c)** small **d)** before **e)** old **f)** opening **g)** downstairs.
3. a) don't live **b)** haven't got **c)** doesn't play **d)** doesn't have **e)** doesn't do **f)** don't listen (!) **g)** don't read.
4. a) Does David go swimming every week **b)** Do they do their homework in the evening? **c)** Does Emma stay in bed? **d)** Do you collect stamps? **e)** Am I a good tennis player?
5. a) Mrs Clay works in a department store at the weekends. **b)** The boys don't play football in the garden on Sunday. **c)** Does Mr Potter wash the car on Sundays?
6.a) had, was not, were **b)** came, did **c)** played, didn't play, lost **d)** rained, took
e) watched didn't like, enjoyed **f)** washed, got, Did you wash.